Living Water

for those who thirst ™

Refreshing Encounters with God's Word

NEW LIVING
TRANSLATION ®

Tyndale House Publishers, Inc.
CAROL STREAM, ILLINOIS

Visit Tyndale's exciting Web site at www.tyndale.com

TYNDALE and Tyndale's quill logo are registered trademarks of Tyndale House Publishers, Inc.

Living Books is a registered trademark of Tyndale House Publishers, Inc.

Living Water for Those Who Thirst

Copyright © 2000 by Tyndale House Publishers, Inc.

Prepared with the assistance of The Livingstone Corporation and staff contributors Valerie Weidemann and Dave Veerman.

Cover design by Cowley Associates

Cover/Interior photo copyright © 2000 by PhotoDisc

ISBN-13: 978-0-8423-4237-7
ISBN-10: 0-8423-4237-0

Printed in the United States of America

09 08 07 06
9   8   7   6

contents

introduction

We are all created with a deep thirst for God in our hearts, an empty longing that only God can satisfy. We try to quench that thirst with so many things—significance, success, comfort, peace, wisdom. But all these things, however good, cannot meet our deepest needs. We often drink deeply at these wells and fountains, coming away with a thirst even deeper than before. Long ago, the prophet Jeremiah brought us God's description of our condition, *"My people have done two evil things: They have forsaken me—the fountain of living water. And they have dug for themselves cracked cisterns that can hold no water at all!"* (Jeremiah 2:13).

At the root of it, we thirst for a closeness to our Creator, who alone can offer us wholeness and peace. Our thirst is one that can only be satisfied by the presence of God in our lives. Jesus once described himself to a woman at a well in Samaria as the true drink we long for. *"People soon become thirsty again after drinking this water. But the water I give them takes away thirst altogether. It becomes a perpetual spring within them, giving them eternal life"* (John 4:13-14). In Jesus, God offers us water that can satisfy our deepest thirst and longing.

Jesus shouted to the crowds, *"If you are thirsty, come to me! If you believe in me, come and drink!"* (John 7:37). The invitation has never been withdrawn. Jesus, God's

Word in human flesh, calls us to come to him. We meet him and drink deeply from him in the pages of God's Word. There God will meet our deepest needs. Whether you thirst for the presence of God himself or for peace, love, hope, and truth, the Bible will answer your need. Come and drink.

This booklet is designed to help lead you to that life-giving water that Jesus offers. It is arranged by topic and weaves together refreshing insights and Scripture that speak to your particular need. Page numbers for the Scripture references refer to the *Living Water* edition of the Holy Bible.

for ACCEPTANCE

In his letter to Jewish exiles, Jeremiah reiterated God's love for them in spite of their disobedience. Jeremiah 31:3 says:

> Long ago the LORD said to Israel: "I have loved you, my people, with an everlasting love. With unfailing love I have drawn you to myself."

When God told Peter to share the gospel with non-Jewish people, it was difficult for him to accept this at first. But he affirmed God's love for all nationalities in Acts 10:34-35.

> Then Peter replied, "I see very clearly that God doesn't show partiality. In every nation he accepts those who fear him and do what is right."

It was unthinkable, even scandalous, for Jews to associate with Gentiles. But Peter reminded all the leaders of the early church in Acts 15:8 that God gave the Gentiles the Holy Spirit, proving God's acceptance of them.

> God, who knows people's hearts, confirmed that he accepts Gentiles by giving them the Holy Spirit, just as he gave him to us.

We're used to people playing favorites. Teachers have *pets*, bosses have *fast-track employees*, and just about everyone has a *best friend*. And remember those days when kids would choose sides for playground games? The *good* players were chosen first, and no one wanted to be chosen last.

Considering our experience, we might assume that God acts the same way—that he favors certain people because of ability, personality, physical attributes, social standing, or some other identifying characteristic. (Peter certainly felt that way—he was sure that Gentiles were unclean.) This assumption may lead us to wonder about God's feelings toward us and, perhaps, even to doubt our relationship with him.

But God revealed the truth to Peter: God doesn't act that way. That is, "God doesn't show partiality" (Acts 10:34). Instead, he accepts people "in every nation." The only qualification for acceptance is that they honor and revere ("fear") him and obey him (Acts 10:35).

Are you feeling rejected, put down, or alone? Know that God accepts you, affirms you, and stands by you. And through his Son, Jesus, he gives you eternal life, regardless of your height, beauty, weight, strength, gender, talent, ability, or nationality. He has chosen and accepted *you*.

FOR FURTHER STUDY
- God accepts anyone who turns to him (Matthew 20:13-16).
  page 748
- God unconditionally accepts you (Hebrews 6:18-19).
  page 937

for ACCOMPLISHMENT

Solomon discovered that even the greatest accomplishments do not bring fulfillment if God is not in a person's life. He summarized his search for the meaning of life in Ecclesiastes 2:11:

> But as I looked at everything I had worked so hard to accomplish, it was all so meaningless. It was like chasing the wind. There was nothing really worthwhile anywhere.

In Ephesians 3:20, Paul affirmed that only God's power enables us to accomplish great things for his Kingdom.

> Now glory be to God! By his mighty power at work within us, he is able to accomplish infinitely more than we would ever dare to ask or hope.

In Matthew 10:39, Jesus revealed that God's values are the opposite of the world's values. Only those things achieved by God's strength have lasting value.

> If you cling to your life, you will lose it; but if you give it up for me, you will find it.

Jesus turns the values of the world upside down. He taught that those who lose their life will find it, the first will be last and the last, first, and those who humble themselves will be exalted.

In contrast, worldly values include winning,

being first, and being recognized. In addition, the world's idea of accomplishment involves money, possessions, and power. No wonder the world finds it difficult to understand and accept Christ. To Jesus, true accomplishment includes forgiveness, peace, purpose, and eternal life.

Comparing yourself against the world's standard, you may not measure up, and you may feel that you have accomplished very little—that you are a failure. Yet, according to God's standard, you stand tall, a glorious success. Regardless of the size of your bank account, house, or pile of earthy goods, you are rich in God's grace. The things you have accomplished because of God's power working through you have lasting value. They will stand the test of time.

FOR FURTHER STUDY
- Attitudes are more important than accomplishments (Ezra 3:12). *page 384*
- You won't find meaning in your accomplishments (Ecclesiastes 1:1-11). *page 526*
- Your accomplishments cannot earn you salvation (Philippians 3:4-7). *pages 913-914*
- Base your self-worth on how God sees you (1 Peter 2:9-10). *page 950*

for ACCOUNTABILITY

When the Pharisees accused Jesus of using the power of Satan to drive out demons, Jesus warned them they would be held accountable for speaking lies. Matthew 12:36 tells us that every person will have to give account for every word and action.

And I tell you this, that you must give an account on judgment day of every idle word you speak.

Paul warned the Christians in Rome of the danger of judging and criticizing one another. He reminded them in Romans 14:12-13 that all Christians will answer to God for how they have lived.

Yes, each of us will have to give a personal account to God. So don't condemn each other anymore. Decide instead to live in such a way that you will not put an obstacle in another Christian's path.

Eternal life is God's promise to all believers, but that doesn't mean we do not need to obey God. Paul tells us in 2 Corinthians 5:10 that Christ will judge us and reward us for the good we have done.

For we must all stand before Christ to be judged. We will each receive whatever we deserve for the good or evil we have done in our bodies.

for ADVICE

Esther 2:15 reveals that Esther relied on the advice
of a wise leader when preparing to present herself
to the king for the first time. As a result, she won
the favor of King Xerxes and all who saw her.

*When it was Esther's turn to go to the king, she
accepted the advice of Hegai, the eunuch in
charge of the harem. She asked for nothing except
what he suggested, and she was admired by everyone who saw her.*

Even King Solomon, the wisest person who ever
lived, understood the importance of seeking
advice from others. In Ecclesiastes 4:13, he put
this truth into perspective.

*It is better to be a poor but wise youth than to be
an old and foolish king who refuses all advice.*

In 1 Corinthians 12:8, Paul teaches that the Holy Spirit gives some people a special ability to give wise advice. We should seek the advice of these people.

To one person the Spirit gives the ability to give wise advice; to another he gives the gift of special knowledge.

FOR FURTHER STUDY

- Leaders should consider the advice of others (Exodus 18:13-26). *page 61*
- Older people often give wise advice (1 Kings 12:1-11). *pages 283-284*
- Stay away from people who give wicked advice (Psalm 1:1). *page 432*
- God's guidance leads to good results (Psalm 73:24). *page 468*
- Wise people seek advice (Proverbs 1:5). *page 507*
- Advice can lead to success (Proverbs 11:14). *page 512*
- Foolish people do not listen to advice (Proverbs 12:15). *page 513*

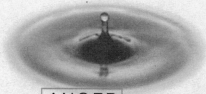

to overcome ANGER

David's advice in Psalm 37:8 highlights the dangers of anger and envy, warning that these destructive emotions lead us away from God and his best for us.

Stop your anger! Turn from your rage! Do not envy others—it only leads to harm.

In Ephesians 4:26-27, Paul tells us not to let anger get a foothold in our life. If we don't deal with anger quickly and properly, it can destroy us.

> *"Don't sin by letting anger gain control over you."*
> *Don't let the sun go down while you are still*
> *angry, for anger gives a mighty foothold to the*
> *Devil.*

Tension in relationships is inevitable, but God's Word encourages us in James 1:19-21 to be patient with one another and "slow to get angry." Angry responses delay healing, but humility and patience go a long way in restoring relationships.

> *My dear brothers and sisters, be quick to listen,*
> *slow to speak, and slow to get angry. Your anger*
> *can never make things right in God's sight. So get*
> *rid of all the filth and evil in your lives, and*
> *humbly accept the message God has planted in*
> *your hearts, for it is strong enough to save your*
> *souls.*

FOR FURTHER STUDY

- Being quick-tempered is foolish (Proverbs 12:16). *page 513*
- Gentle words can soothe anger (Proverbs 15:1). *page 514*
- Despising someone is like murdering them (Matthew 5:21-22). *page 732*
- Jesus became angry at sin (John 2:13-17). *page 813*
- Christians should get rid of anger and rage (Colossians 3:8). *page 917*
- Leaders in the church should not be quick-tempered (Titus 1:7). *page 931*

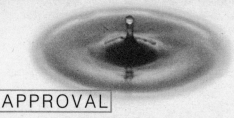

for APPROVAL

In Psalm 90, Moses contrasts God's eternal, perfect character with the temporal, flawed character of human beings. Moses concludes the psalm with a prayer in verse 17, asking for God's approval. Moses understood that God's approval is all that matters because he alone brings success.

And may the Lord our God show us his approval and make our efforts successful. Yes, make our efforts successful!

Proverbs 8 portrays wisdom as a woman who guides people and brings them success. Verse 35 explains that God approves of those who seek and apply wisdom.

For whoever finds me finds life and wins approval from the LORD.

Bible knowledge is not enough to gain God's approval—we need to let God's word sink into our hearts and become part of our daily lives. Romans 2:13 clearly states that God desires obedience, not merely knowledge.

For it is not merely knowing the law that brings God's approval. Those who obey the law will be declared right in God's sight.

- No one can earn God's approval (1 Corinthians 8:8). *page 884*
- God's approval comes as a gift, received through Jesus Christ (Galatians 2:19). *page 903*
- God gives his approval to people because of their faith (Hebrews 11:2, 39). *pages 941-942*

for ASSURANCE

The psalm writer acknowledged that the needs of the poor had been ignored and their situation seemed hopeless. But Psalm 9:18 states that their God had not forgotten them—he would care for them.

For the needy will not be forgotten forever; the hopes of the poor will not always be crushed.

God assured his people through the prophet Jeremiah that he would be faithful to them and accomplish his ultimate plan through them. Jeremiah 32:40-41 gives his wonderful promise:

"I will make an everlasting covenant with them, promising not to stop doing good for them. I will put a desire in their hearts to worship me, and they will never leave me. I will rejoice in doing good to them and will faithfully and wholeheartedly replant them in this land."

In this letter to the believers in Rome, Paul assures Christians everywhere of God's never-ending love for them. He writes in Romans 8:38-39:

*I am convinced that nothing can ever separate us
from his love. Death can't, and life can't. The
angels can't, and the demons can't. Our fears for
today, our worries about tomorrow, and even the
powers of hell can't keep God's love away.
Whether we are high above the sky or in the deepest ocean, nothing in all creation will ever be able
to separate us from the love of God that is revealed
in Christ Jesus our Lord.*

Remember when you were a child and became
separated from your mother in the department
store? All you saw were tall strangers and
merchandise stacked to the ceiling as you
panicked and rushed from aisle to aisle. Few
things are as frightening as the feeling of being
lost or abandoned.

Even as adults, however, we can still feel forgotten and lost at times, and this leaves us feeling
vulnerable and afraid. In these times, we need to
listen to God's Word, which is packed with promises of God's everlasting love for those who trust
him. Although you may seem virtually invisible in
this world, God sees you—he has not forgotten or
abandoned you. Although the future looks dismal
today, we can always count on God's promise to
be with us.

You are not lost—look up and find God. And
look ahead, to eternity, and find hope.

FOR FURTHER STUDY
- God always holds onto his children (Psalm 37:23-24).
  page 449
- God will never abandon his people (Psalm 138:8).
  page 501
- God will not refuse any who come to him (John 6:37-40).
  page 818

for BEAUTY

First Peter 3:3-4 states that we should spend more of our time cultivating our character than worrying about our outward appearance.

> *Don't be concerned about the outward beauty that depends on fancy hairstyles, expensive jewelry, or beautiful clothes. You should be known for the beauty that comes from within, the unfading beauty of a gentle and quiet spirit, which is so precious to God.*

God sent Samuel to Bethlehem to anoint one of Jesse's sons as the next king of Israel. Samuel assumed the next king would be tall, handsome, and strong, but God chose the youngest son— David, a shepherd boy. 1 Samuel 16:7 reveals the Lord's reasoning:

> *People judge by outward appearance, but the LORD looks at a person's thoughts and intentions.*

12

Over the centuries, society has continued to value superficial appearances. Plaudits and power still come to the beautiful people—sports stars and media celebrities with exceptional physical characteristics. With such men and women presented as ideals and models, it's easy for the rest of us to feel ugly, unwanted, insignificant, and worthless in comparison.

But God's standards have not changed. Rather than outward appearance, he looks at the inside of a person, examining thoughts and intentions, desires, motives, character, attitudes, and faith.

Expend your energy on developing inner beauty. That's what matters to God. And his opinion of us is what matters most.

FOR FURTHER STUDY
- The gift of beauty can lead to pride (Ezekiel 28:17). *page 650*
- Physical beauty fades (Proverbs 31:30). *page 525*
- Appearances can be deceiving (Matthew 23:27). *page 752*
- Beauty comes in many different forms (1 Corinthians 15:41). *page 891*
- Inner beauty should be your priority (1 Timothy 2:9-10). *page 925*
- Do not judge people by their outward appearance (James 2:2-4). *page 945*

for BELONGING

Leviticus 26:12 makes an astounding claim. The God of the universe wants us to be his people. He wants us to know that we belong to him.

I will walk among you; I will be your God, and you will be my people.

First John 2:3-4 makes it very clear. Those who belong to God will be marked by obedience to God's commandments.

And how can we be sure that we belong to him? By obeying his commandments. If someone says, "I belong to God," but doesn't obey God's commandments, that person is a liar and does not live in the truth.

Through the prophet Isaiah, God promised the people of Judah that he would be with them in every circumstance and through every trial. Isaiah 43:1-3 states:

"Do not be afraid, for I have ransomed you. I have called you by name; you are mine. When you go through deep waters and great trouble, I will be with you. When you go through rivers of difficulty, you will not drown! When you walk through the fire of oppression, you will not be burned up; the flames will not consume you. For I am the LORD, your God, the Holy One of Israel, your Savior."

God promised to be with his people through the good times and the bad times. He had ransomed and called his people, and he would keep them safe and secure. They were *his*. They belonged to him.

You, too, are God's child. You belong to God and can claim these promises for yourself.

What deep waters of tragedy and sorrow do you face? You are not alone—God is with you.

What rivers of conflict and difficulty swirl around you, threatening to engulf you and carry you away? Don't fear—God will lead you through.

What fire licks at your heels? Keep walking— God will shield you from the flames.

Keep on, knowing that you *belong* to God, the Holy One, your Savior.

FOR FURTHER STUDY
- You belong to God, who is your refuge (Deuteronomy 33:27). *page 175*
- You belong to the Lord, the good shepherd (Psalm 23:1-6). *page 442*
- God cares deeply for each one who belongs to him (Luke 15:3-7). *page 800*
- Belonging to Christ can bring persecution (John 15:19-21). *page 828*
- Believers belong to Christ's body, the Church (Romans 12:4-5). *page 875*

for BLESSING

Second Samuel 7:29 records David's humble prayer accepting God's rich blessing on him and his descendants.

"And now, may it please you to bless me and my family so that our dynasty may continue forever before you. For when you grant a blessing to your servant, O Sovereign LORD, it is an eternal blessing!"

Proverbs 10:22 reveals that God's blessing on a person's life brings fulfillment and satisfaction.

The blessing of the LORD makes a person rich, and he adds no sorrow with it.

God promised to bless the people of Israel, just as he had blessed Noah generations earlier. Isaiah 54:10 is a promise all of God's people can claim for their own.

"For the mountains may depart and the hills disappear, but even then I will remain loyal to you. My covenant of blessing will never be broken," says the LORD, who has mercy on you.

In Numbers 6:24-26, God instructed Aaron and his sons to pronounce this special blessing on the people of Israel:

'May the LORD bless you and protect you. May the LORD smile on you and be gracious to you. May

the LORD show you his favor and give you his peace.'

This passage in Numbers 6 is a familiar benediction that often graces church services. Whether sung by the choir or pronounced by the pastor, it gives the congregation a comfortable, warm feeling as they exit. Unfortunately, much like the expression "God bless you" after a sneeze, this benediction has become trivialized by familiarity. We really don't think much about the rich and plentiful blessings God has given us.

But consider these statements:

Protect you—requesting God's protection and guidance

Smile on you—requesting a close, loving relationship with God

Be gracious—requesting that God would shower his forgiveness and kindness upon you, though unearned and undeserved

Give you his peace—requesting inner strength, resolve, and confidence for living in tumultuous times

Certainly this blessing of the Israelites contains much of what we really want God to do in our lives. But the key statement lies in verse 27: This "will designate the Israelites as my people."

Do you belong to God? Do you bear his name? This passage is for you. Know that you are *blessed!*

FOR FURTHER STUDY
- God blesses those who obey him (Leviticus 26:3-5). *page 105*
- God blesses godly people (Psalm 5:12). *page 433*
- You are blessed when you worship God (Psalm 24:3-6). *page 442*

- Christians bless God through praise (Psalm 103:1).
  page 483
- God will bless those who fear him (Psalm 112:1-3).
  page 490
- God blesses you when you seek to please him (Matthew 6:33). *page 734*
- Christians should bless their enemies (Luke 6:28).
  page 788
- Salvation is the greatest blessing (Ephesians 1:3).
  page 907
- Obeying God's law brings blessing (James 1:25).
  page 945

for God's CARE

When her husband refused hospitality to David and his men, Abigail encouraged David with these words in 1 Samuel 25:29. She saved David from making a foolish mistake by reminding him of God's care.

"Even when you are chased by those who seek your life, you are safe in the care of the LORD your God, secure in his treasure pouch!"

In Psalm 37, David contrasts the wicked person and the righteous person. Verses 17 and 18 declare that God faithfully cares for the righteous—they can count on the Lord in their time of need.

For the strength of the wicked will be shattered, but the LORD takes care of the godly. Day by day

> the LORD takes care of the innocent, and they will
> receive a reward that lasts forever.

Matthew 10:29-31 assures us of our value in God's
sight. We can be confident of his care for us
because he loves us.

> [Jesus said] "Not even a sparrow, worth only half a
> penny, can fall to the ground without your Father
> knowing it. And the very hairs on your head are all
> numbered. So don't be afraid; you are more valu-
> able to him than a whole flock of sparrows."

One of the smallest birds is the sparrow—and
surely one of the most common and ordinary.
Sparrows come in many varieties and can be
found all over the world.

Jesus used this tiny and seemingly insignificant
creature to illustrate God's care for the earth and
to teach the value of God's most cherished
creation—human beings.

How much are sparrows worth? In the world,
not very much. But God knows when each one
falls. How much are you worth . . .

According to the world?

According to God?

Whenever you feel hopeless, helpless, and
worthless, consider that you hold much more
value than any sparrow. God knows you, watches
you, and deeply cares for you.

FOR FURTHER STUDY
- God cares for his people (Deuteronomy 7:9). *page 152*
- God cares for underprivileged people (Psalm 68:5).
  page 463
- God's people should protect the needy (Psalm 82:3).
  page 473

- God's people should help the oppressed (Isaiah 1:17).
  page 537
- God's people should care for the needy (Luke 14:13-14).
  page 799

to cope with CHANGE

Peter offered this encouragement to suffering Christians. One thing would never change—they could count on receiving their spiritual inheritance. First Peter 1:4 promises:

For God has reserved a priceless inheritance for his children. It is kept in heaven for you, pure and undefiled, beyond the reach of change and decay.

Hebrews 6:17 assures believers that in the midst of unsettling change, they can be sure that two things will never change: God's character and his promises.

God also bound himself with an oath, so that those who received the promise could be perfectly sure that he would never change his mind.

Hebrews 13:8 proclaims that Jesus is unlike all human leaders in that he never changes—he has proven his faithfulness throughout generations.

Jesus Christ is the same yesterday, today, and forever.

Change defines our world. Each day, a dazzling array of changes confronts us. Governments fall, children grow and mature, friends move away, storms uproot trees, new buildings replace old ones, colors fade, summer turns into fall, and technological advances render modern appliances obsolete. All these changes tend to undermine our feelings of security—we wonder what will last, what is solid, and who will be there.

Then we turn to God's Word, which proclaims the reassuring fact that our God does not change. In truth, he is the same as he has always been—loving, forgiving, merciful, and just. And, unlike the sources of many of our disappointments, God is reliable—he keeps his promises. We can be sure that what he says, he will do. We can know that he will be with us and for us in the future, forever, in fact, just as he is today.

Feeling unsure or insecure as you face the continuous onslaught of change? Plant your feet and your faith on a solid foundation—your unchanging Lord.

FOR FURTHER STUDY
- God does not change his mind (Numbers 23:19). *page 132*
- God is faithful (1 Samuel 15:29). *page 233*
- God's decrees never change (Psalm 119:152). *page 496*
- God's Spirit can change your heart (Romans 2:29). *page 866*

to develop CHARACTER

Why would we *rejoice* when we encounter problems? The Bible tells us in Romans 5:3-4 that life's difficulties are opportunities to grow and strengthen character.

> *We can rejoice, too, when we run into problems and trials, for we know that they are good for us— they help us learn to endure. And endurance develops strength of character in us, and character strengthens our confident expectation of salvation.*

You won't know the depth of your character until it is tested. James 1:3-4 teaches that God allows pain and problems to help his people grow in maturity. The key is to turn to God in our tough times and rely on him for endurance.

> *For when your faith is tested, your endurance has a chance to grow. So let it grow, for when your endurance is fully developed, you will be strong in character and ready for anything.*

FOR FURTHER STUDY
- Difficult times provide opportunities to prove your character (Deuteronomy 8:2). *page 153*
- God sometimes tests a person's character (Psalm 105:19). *page 485*
- Bad company corrupts good character (1 Corinthians 15:33). *page 890*

- A person should prove his or her good character before becoming a church leader (1 Timothy 3:10). *page 925*

for CHRIST'S RETURN

Jesus said that even he did not know the time of his return, but that when it happened, it would be unmistakable. Mark 13:26-27 describes a day that all believers can anticipate eagerly and joyfully:

> *[Jesus said] "Then everyone will see the Son of Man arrive on the clouds with great power and glory. And he will send forth his angels to gather together his chosen ones from all over the world—from the farthest ends of the earth and heaven."*

Jesus is preparing a beautiful place for us to reign with him for all eternity. In John 14:2-4, he promises to return for us to take us to that wondrous place.

> *"There are many rooms in my Father's home, and I am going to prepare a place for you. If this were not so, I would tell you plainly. When everything is ready, I will come and get you, so that you will always be with me where I am. And you know where I am going and how to get there."*

After spending forty days with his disciples, Jesus ascended to heaven. Angels reassured his followers that Jesus would return in the same way he left. Acts 1:9-11 describes the scene:

It was not long after he said this that he was taken up into the sky while they were watching, and he disappeared into a cloud. As they were straining their eyes to see him, two white-robed men suddenly stood there among them. They said, "Men of Galilee, why are you standing here staring at the sky? Jesus has been taken away from you into heaven. And someday, just as you saw him go, he will return!"

Why did the disciples stand and look intently into the sky? Maybe they were stunned and amazed at seeing Jesus ascend into the air through the clouds. They may have been saddened by his sudden disappearance and were looking anxiously for him to descend. Or perhaps they were confused and didn't know what else to do.

Whatever their thought or motives, however, two angels gave them the message they needed to hear. They could stop looking *up* and start looking *around* at the world and its needy people. They could stop waiting and start working to fulfill Christ's commission. They could stop wondering and start living with the assurance that Jesus would come again, just as he had promised.

Although nearly two thousand years have passed since this dramatic event, the angels' message still stands—Jesus will surely return. That truth should continue to motivate believers. In fact, each day that passes provides another day to work for Christ and his Kingdom.

Keep hoping, working, loving, sharing the Good News, and living for the Savior. He will come back.

FOR FURTHER STUDY

to serve in the CHURCH

If you serve in the church out of love for God and through the power of the Holy Spirit, God will be pleased and accept your service as a gift of worship to him. Romans 14:17-19 describes this kind of service:

> *For the Kingdom of God is not a matter of what we eat or drink, but of living a life of goodness and peace and joy in the Holy Spirit. If you serve*

Christ with this attitude, you will please God. And other people will approve of you, too. So then, let us aim for harmony in the church and try to build each other up.

Paul recommends in 1 Timothy 3:10 that positions of leadership in the church should be given only to those who have proven themselves to be good workers. If we do our best at whatever jobs we're given in the church, God will use us!

Before they are appointed as deacons, they should be given other responsibilities in the church as a test of their character and ability. If they do well, then they may serve as deacons.

FOR FURTHER STUDY

- Jesus is the cornerstone of the church (Psalm 118:22). *page 492*
- Believers should enjoy going to God's house (Psalm 122:1). *page 496*
- Members of the church should take care of each other (Acts 2:44). *page 837*
- The church sends out missionaries (Acts 13:2). *page 847*
- The church is like a human body (1 Corinthians 12:12-13). *page 887*
- The church is a family of Christians (Galatians 6:10). *page 906*
- God's children form the church (Ephesians 2:19-22). *page 908*
- The church should not allow immoral behavior by members (Ephesians 5:3-4). *page 910*
- Christ is the head of the church (Colossians 1:18). *page 917*
- The universal church is made up of Christians of all ethnicities (Colossians 3:11). *page 918*
- Church leaders are qualified by their character (Titus 1:6-9). *page 931*

- The church is made up of God's children (1 John 3:1).
  page 957
- The church is the bride of Christ (Revelation 19:7-8).
  page 975

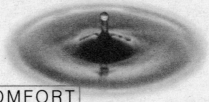

for COMFORT

Following a victory over the Philistines, David remembered that God hears cries for help. He wrote in Psalm 9:9-10:

> *The LORD is a shelter for the oppressed, a refuge in times of trouble. Those who know your name trust in you, for you, O LORD, have never abandoned anyone who searches for you.*

Just before his arrest, trial, and crucifixion, Jesus encouraged his disciples with this profound promise in John 14:1-3:

> *"Don't be troubled. You trust God, now trust in me. There are many rooms in my Father's home, and I am going to prepare a place for you. If this were not so, I would tell you plainly. When everything is ready, I will come and get you, so that you will always be with me where I am."*

In writing to the church at Corinth, Paul highlighted this hopeful promise of God's mercy and comfort. Second Corinthians 1:3-7 states:

> *All praise to the God and Father of our Lord Jesus Christ. He is the source of every mercy and the God who comforts us. He comforts us in all our*

troubles so that we can comfort others. When others are troubled, we will be able to give them the same comfort God has given us. You can be sure that the more we suffer for Christ, the more God will shower us with his comfort through Christ. So when we are weighed down with troubles, it is for your benefit and salvation! For when God comforts us, it is so that we, in turn, can be an encouragement to you. Then you can patiently endure the same things we suffer. We are confident that as you share in suffering, you will also share God's comfort.

Many think that when God comforts us, our hardships should go away. But if that were always so, people would turn to God only to be relieved of pain and not out of love for him. We must understand that *comfort* can also mean receiving strength, encouragement, and hope to deal with our hardships. The more we suffer, the more comfort God gives us. If you are feeling overwhelmed, allow God to comfort you as only he can. And remember that every trial you endure will later become an opportunity to minister to other people suffering similar hardships.

FOR FURTHER STUDY

- Friends should comfort each other (Job 2:12-13). *page 413*
- God comforts his children in their darkest times (Job 35:10). *page 428*
- God desires to comfort his people (Isaiah 40:1-11). *page 561*
- God promises to comfort those who mourn (Matthew 5:4). *page 732*
- God's Holy Spirit is the Comforter (John 14:16). *page 827*
- Jesus has overcome the world's troubles (John 16:33). *page 829*

- Christians should comfort each other (1 Thessalonians 4:18). *page 921*
- One day all pain will end (Revelation 21:3-4). *page 976*

for COMMUNITY

David declares the joy of harmonious relationships in Psalm 133:1. Striving for a sense of unity and community with others is worth the effort.

> *How wonderful it is, how pleasant, when brothers live together in harmony!*

The Christian life should not be lived in isolation. Philippians 2:1-2 tells us that the church is a spiritual community that can support us and help us grow in our faith.

> *Is there any encouragement from belonging to Christ? Any comfort from his love? Any fellowship together in the Spirit? Are your hearts tender and sympathetic? Then make me truly happy by agreeing wholeheartedly with each other, loving one another, and working together with one heart and purpose.*

Jesus promised to send the Holy Spirit to help his followers stay united in their faith. John 17:11 is a promise to claim today:

> *"Now I am departing the world; I am leaving them behind and coming to you. Holy Father,*

*keep them and care for them—all those you have
given me—so that they will be united just as we
are."*

FOR FURTHER STUDY
- God's people should celebrate together (Exodus 12:47).
  page 56
- Believers should bear one another's joys and burdens
  (Romans 12:9-16). *page 875*
- Believers must seek unity in all essentials (1 Corinthians
  1:10). *page 879*
- There can be great unity even in great diversity (Ephesians
  4:3-13). *page 909*

for COMPASSION

God's compassion for us is greater than we can
imagine! Isaiah 30:18 describes God's *eagerness* for
us to go to him for comfort and love.

> *But the LORD still waits for you to come to him so
> he can show you his love and compassion. For the
> LORD is a faithful God. Blessed are those who
> wait for him to help them.*

When Jesus heard that John the Baptist had been
beheaded by Herod, he withdrew to a private
place to grieve, pray, and rest. But the crowds
followed him relentlessly. How did Jesus respond
to the throng of needy people? Matthew 14:13-14
tells us that he had compassion on them and
ministered to them.

As soon as Jesus heard the news, he went off by himself in a boat to a remote area to be alone. But the crowds heard where he was headed and followed by land from many villages. A vast crowd was there as he stepped from the boat, and he had compassion on them and healed their sick.

In the parable of the lost son, Jesus portrays God as a patient, loving, welcoming, compassionate father. Luke 15:20 assures us that God has compassion on us, even when we turn against him.

"So he returned home to his father. And while he was still a long distance away, his father saw him coming. Filled with love and compassion, he ran to his son, embraced him, and kissed him."

FOR FURTHER STUDY

- God has proven his compassion throughout history (Psalm 25:6). *page 442*
- God saves people because of his compassion (Psalm 135:14). *page 500*
- God has compassion on you in your time of need (Isaiah 49:13). *page 568*
- Jesus showed compassion for people (Luke 7:13). *page 789*

for CONFIDENCE

Throughout history, God has proven himself trustworthy and dependable. Psalm 118:8-9 declares the wisdom of putting our full confidence in him.

31

> *It is better to trust the LORD than to put confidence in people. It is better to trust the LORD than to put confidence in princes.*

Proverbs 25:19 gives us a vivid picture of how foolish it is to put our confidence in people. People will always fail us, but God never will.

> *Putting confidence in an unreliable person is like chewing with a toothache or walking on a broken foot.*

FOR FURTHER STUDY
- It is foolish to put your confidence in people, even powerful people (Psalm 146:3). *page 504*
- God will help you if you put your confidence in him (Isaiah 30:15). *page 554*
- God blesses those who put their confidence in him (Jeremiah 17:7). *page 592*
- Over-confidence in yourself is wrong (Luke 18:9). *page 803*

for help in resolving CONFLICT

In his letter to the Corinthians, Paul encourages believers to work on resolving their disagreements and problems. He reminds us in 1 Corinthians 6:3 that we are not helpless—we can depend on the power of the Holy Spirit to resolve conflicts.

> *Don't you realize that we Christians will judge angels? So you should surely be able to resolve ordinary disagreements here on earth.*

When Paul and his companions arrived in Macedonia, they were bombarded with problems. But 2 Corinthians 7:5-6 reveals that God encouraged them through a friend named Titus. Likewise, God will help us through our difficulties.

When we arrived in Macedonia there was no rest for us. Outside there was conflict from every direction, and inside there was fear. But God, who encourages those who are discouraged, encouraged us by the arrival of Titus.

FOR FURTHER STUDY
- Unresolved conflict can end friendships (Proverbs 18:18-19). *page 517*
- God wants believers to live in harmony with each other (Romans 12:16). *page 875*
- Christians should build each other up (Romans 14:19). *page 876*
- Conflict is reduced when people live unselfishly (Philippians 2:3). *page 913*
- Avoid foolish arguments (2 Timothy 2:23). *page 929*

for a clear CONSCIENCE

A person's conscience remains sensitive as long as he *listens* to it. Proverbs 28:13-14 encourages us to admit when we have made a mistake and learn from it.

People who cover over their sins will not prosper. But if they confess and forsake them, they will receive mercy. Blessed are those who have a tender conscience, but the stubborn are headed for serious trouble.

First Timothy 1:19 reminds us that the conscience is a blessing from God. Our faith will be strengthened as we work hard to keep a clear conscience.

Cling tightly to your faith in Christ, and always keep your conscience clear. For some people have deliberately violated their consciences; as a result, their faith has been shipwrecked.

FOR FURTHER STUDY
- The conscience can be suppressed (Jonah 1:5). *page 701*
- The Holy Spirit can speak through a person's conscience (Romans 9:1). *page 872*
- Church leaders must have clear consciences (1 Timothy 3:9). *page 925*
- Consciences can be destroyed (1 Timothy 4:2). *page 925*
- Jesus' forgiveness clears the conscience (Hebrews 9:14). *page 939*
- A clear conscience will help you live a God-honoring life (1 Peter 3:16). *page 951*

for CONTENTMENT

Paul had learned the secret of contentment. He wrote in Philippians 4:11-13 that whether we have a lot or a little, the key is to depend on God and his strength.

Not that I was ever in need, for I have learned

how to get along happily whether I have much or little. I know how to live on almost nothing or with everything. I have learned the secret of living in every situation, whether it is with a full stomach or empty, with plenty or little. For I can do everything with the help of Christ who gives me the strength I need.

Paul challenged young Timothy to strive for contentment regardless of his circumstances. He wrote in 1 Timothy 6:6-8:

Yet true religion with contentment is great wealth. After all, we didn't bring anything with us when we came into the world, and we certainly cannot carry anything with us when we die. So if we have enough food and clothing, let us be content.

More, more, more! The world bombards us with messages telling us we need: more money, more power, more gadgets, more luxuries, more status. It is easy to believe that the next thing, just beyond our reach, will bring us happiness. But when we finally attain it, the thrill fades quickly. Greed traps us in an endless cycle that results in pain and heartache. How can we escape the grip of our desires?

Paul offers some practical help. He contends that true fulfillment comes through a personal relationship with Jesus Christ and aligning our desires with Christ's priorities. Jesus offers us contentment and peace of mind that the world's greatest riches can never bring.

Instead of focusing on the things you do not have, focus on the blessings God has given you. Thank him for his generous gifts to you. And rely on Christ's power to be content in all circumstances.

for COURAGE

God does not promise to protect us from problems, but he will give us the courage to face our problems in his strength. Jesus encouraged and inspired his followers with these words in John 16:33:

> *"I have told you all this so that you may have peace in me. Here on earth you will have many trials and sorrows. But take heart, because I have overcome the world."*

When the church in Corinth faced some difficult problems, the apostle Paul wrote them a letter reminding them to be strong and courageous in the Lord. First Corinthians 16:13 says:

> *Be on guard. Stand true to what you believe. Be courageous. Be strong.*

- Gideon displayed courage through faith (Judges 7:1-25).
  pages 204-205
- Courage helps you to boldly represent Christ (Acts 4:31).
  page 839
- Pray for courage (Ephesians 6:19-20). *page 911*
- Christians can pray with confidence (Hebrews 4:16). *page 936*

for CREATIVITY

Genesis 1:1 and the entire creation story reveals God's creativity. He is the Master Creator who delights in diversity and variety.

In the beginning God created the heavens and the earth.

Creativity is a gift God gives to people by the power of his Holy Spirit. Exodus 31:1-4 describes a person who used his artistic skills and craftsmanship to make beautiful things for God's glory.

The LORD also said to Moses, "Look, I have chosen Bezalel son of Uri, grandson of Hur, of the tribe of Judah. I have filled him with the Spirit of God, giving him great wisdom, intelligence, and skill in all kinds of crafts. He is able to create beautiful objects from gold, silver, and bronze.

Hebrews 11:3 proclaims God as the ultimate source of all creativity.

By faith we understand that the entire universe

*was formed at God's command, that what we now
see did not come from anything that can be seen.*

FOR FURTHER STUDY

- Creation displays God's creativity (Genesis 1:2-27).
  page 3
- God wants you to use your creativity (Genesis 2:19-20).
  page 4
- You can use your creativity for God's glory (Exodus 35:32).
  page 76
- Creativity can be destructive when used wrongly (Isaiah
  44:16-17). *page 565*

for help in dealing with

CRITICISM

A wise person receives criticism in humility and
tries to learn from it. Proverbs 13:18 contrasts the
results of ignoring criticism and accepting it.

> *If you ignore criticism, you will end in poverty and
> disgrace; if you accept criticism, you will be
> honored.*

Not all criticism is helpful. Proverbs 15:31-32
encourages us to listen to *constructive* criticism, the
advice that helps us grow and mature.

> *If you listen to constructive criticism, you will be
> at home among the wise. If you reject criticism,
> you only harm yourself; but if you listen to correc-
> tion, you grow in understanding.*

Harsh criticism can destroy a person's self worth. Galatians 5:15 admonishes believers to avoid being over-critical. Love should characterize our relationships.

> *But if instead of showing love among yourselves you are always biting and devouring one another, watch out! Beware of destroying one another.*

FOR FURTHER STUDY
- Respond properly to an insult (Proverbs 12:16). *page 513*
- Take care of your own problems before criticizing others (Matthew 7:3-5). *page 734*
- God will bless Christians who are mocked because of their faith (Luke 6:22). *page 788*
- Criticism should be used to help people obey God better (Luke 17:3). *page 802*
- Criticism should be given with a loving attitude (1 Corinthians 13:4). *page 888*
- Do not insult others (1 Peter 3:9). *page 951*

for help making DECISIONS

When Nehemiah learned that the walls of Jerusalem had been torn down and the returned exiles were in trouble, he turned to God for help. His first reaction when faced with bad news was to ask God for wisdom in deciding his response. Nehemiah 1:4-5 and 11 says:

> *When I heard this, I sat down and wept. In fact, for days I mourned, fasted, and prayed to the God*

of heaven. Then I said, "O LORD, God of heaven, the great and awesome God who keeps his covenant of unfailing love with those who love him and obey his commands. O Lord, please hear my prayer! Listen to the prayers of those of us who delight in honoring you. Please grant me success now as I go to ask the king for a great favor. Put it into his heart to be kind to me."

Paul warns believers in 2 Corinthians 10:7 of the danger of making decisions based on appearances. God can help us see what is true and real, thus enabling us to make wise choices.

The trouble with you is that you make your decisions on the basis of appearance. You must recognize that we belong to Christ just as much as those who proudly declare that they belong to Christ.

James 1:5-8 holds a wonderful promise for all believers: God will give us all the wisdom we need to make good decisions, if we ask expectantly and in faith.

If you need wisdom—if you want to know what God wants you to do—ask him, and he will gladly tell you. He will not resent your asking. But when you ask him, be sure that you really expect him to answer, for a doubtful mind is as unsettled as a wave of the sea that is driven and tossed by the wind. People like that should not expect to receive anything from the Lord. They can't make up their minds. They waver back and forth in everything they do.

FOR FURTHER STUDY
- Decide to do things that honor God (Job 1:8). *page 412*
- God's Word helps you makes decisions (Psalm 119:105). *page 495*

40

• Get good advice before making decisions (Proverbs 18:15). *page 517*

to overcome DEPRESSION

David received God's healing from depression. In Psalm 30:11, he praises God for turning his sorrow and grief into joy.

> *You have turned my mourning into joyful dancing. You have taken away my clothes of mourning and clothed me with joy.*

The psalmist discovered that God's Word can bring joy in the midst of distress. He encourages us in Psalm 119:143 to turn to God and his Word for healing and comfort.

> *As pressure and stress bear down on me, I find joy in your commands.*

Revelation 21:3-4 holds words of promise for those who feel hopeless about their emotional state. The apostle John describes a place where there will be no death, pain, sorrow, crying, or depression. Believers will enjoy eternity in this perfect place with God forever.

> *I heard a loud shout from the throne, saying, "Look, the home of God is now among his people! He will live with them, and they will be his people. God himself will be with them. He will remove all of their sorrows, and there will be no*

more death or sorrow or crying or pain. For the old world and its evils are gone forever."

FOR FURTHER STUDY
- Depression can follow exhausting times (Judges 15:18). *page 212*
- God can encourage hurting people (2 Samuel 22:29). *page 266*
- Depression can follow success (1 Kings 19:3-4). *page 291*
- God helps those who feel crushed (Psalm 34:18). *page 447*
- Abraham had hope when there was no reason to hope (Romans 4:18-22). *page 868*

for DIRECTION

Psalm 37:23 offers a reassuring promise of God's direction in our lives.

> *The steps of the godly are directed by the LORD. He delights in every detail of their lives.*

Life is confusing. Proverbs 20:24 counsels us to trust God for guidance—he is the one who knows our future and controls the details of our life.

> *How can we understand the road we travel? It is the LORD who directs our steps.*

God's Word is the best source for direction in life. Proverbs 29:18 promises happiness to those who seek and obey God's guidance.

> *When people do not accept divine guidance, they run wild. But whoever obeys the law is happy.*

for help in coping with
DISAPPOINTMENT

David knew disappointment—his friends had rejected and abandoned him in his time of need. But David turned to God in his despair. He believed that God would come through for him and meet his needs. Psalm 22:5 says:

You heard their cries for help and saved them. They put their trust in you and were never disappointed.

In times of disappointment, be thankful that God will never let you down. Romans 10:11 promises:

Anyone who believes in him will not be disappointed.

- You will not be disappointed in the future God has prepared for you (Proverbs 23:18). *page 520*
- An eternal perspective will help you cope with disappointment (Galatians 6:9). *page 906*

for DISCERNMENT

The Bereans serve as a model to follow—when they encountered new ideas and faced decisions of faith, they searched God's Word to help them discern the truth. Their story in Acts 17:11 encourages us to turn to the Bible for help whenever we need discernment.

And the people of Berea were more open-minded than those in Thessalonica, and they listened eagerly to Paul's message. They searched the Scriptures day after day to check up on Paul and Silas, to see if they were really teaching the truth.

First Corinthians 12:10 reveals that the Holy Spirit gives some believers the gift of discernment, a special ability to discern truth from falsehood. If you need help, seek the advice of someone who has demonstrated this gift.

He gives one person the power to perform miracles, and to another the ability to prophesy. He gives someone else the ability to know whether it is really the Spirit of God or another spirit that is speaking. Still another person is given the ability to speak in unknown languages, and another is given the ability to interpret what is being said.

FOR FURTHER STUDY
- Believers should pray for discernment (Psalm 119:125).
  page 495
- Seek wisdom and discernment from God (Proverbs 23:23).
  page 520
- Discern between right and wrong behavior (Hebrews 5:14).
  page 936
- Ask God for help in discerning his will (James 1:5). *page 945*

to overcome
DISCOURAGEMENT

One antidote for discouragement is to focus on God's goodness and his ability to help us through life's difficulties. When feeling discouraged, we should take hold of the hope and promise in Psalm 42:11.

Why am I discouraged? Why so sad? I will put my hope in God! I will praise him again—my Savior and my God!

When we feel discouraged, we can claim Galatians 6:9 as a promise from God. He will help us and bless us if we put our hope in him.

So don't get tired of doing what is good. Don't get discouraged and give up, for we will reap a harvest of blessing at the appropriate time.

FOR FURTHER STUDY
• Discouragement can cause people to turn away from God (Exodus 6:9). *page 50*
• God promises his help during hard times (Deuteronomy 31:8). *page 171*
• Discouragement can open you up to attack (2 Samuel 17:2). *page 260*
• Remembering God's goodness helps you cope with discouragement (Psalm 42:5). *page 452*

to avoid DISOBEDIENCE

Avoiding disobedience is easier when we saturate our minds with God's Word. Psalm 119:39-40 highlights the importance and power of God's Word:

> *Help me abandon my shameful ways; your laws are all I want in life. I long to obey your commandments! Renew my life with your goodness.*

No one is perfect—everyone fails. But Romans 4:7-8 describes the joy we can experience when we confess our disobedience and receive God's abundant forgiveness.

> *"Oh, what joy for those whose disobedience is forgiven, whose sins are put out of sight. Yes, what joy for those whose sin is no longer counted against them by the Lord."*

Paul admonishes believers to place their sinful desires under Christ's control. First Thessalonians

46

4:7-8 reminds us that we can receive power
through the Holy Spirit to avoid disobedience.

> *God has called us to be holy, not to live impure
> lives. Anyone who refuses to live by these rules is
> not disobeying human rules but is rejecting God,
> who gives his Holy Spirit to you.*

FOR FURTHER STUDY

- Disobedience has consequences (Deuteronomy 4:26).
  page 150
- God punishes disobedience (Joshua 23:15). *page 196*
- Disobedience separates a person from God and his bless-
  ings (2 Chronicles 24:20). *page 369*
- God hates disobedience (Ephesians 5:6). *page 910*
- Persistent prayer helps you avoid disobedience (Ephesians
  6:18). *page 918*
- The Holy Spirit helps you avoid disobedience (2 Timothy
  1:13-14). *page 928*
- Jesus shows how to avoid disobedience (Hebrews 5:8).
  page 936

to overcome DOUBT

Doubting is not wrong if it helps us turn to God.
Psalm 94:19 assures us that God draws near to us
when we feel unsure and afraid; he brings us joy
and hope.

> *When doubts filled my mind, your comfort gave
> me renewed hope and cheer.*

Isaiah 40:27-28 reminds us of God's trustworthy
character—He *sees* us, he *hears* us, and he will *help*

us. God remains the same even when we are filled with doubt.

O Israel, how can you say the LORD does not see your troubles? How can you say God refuses to hear your case? Have you never heard or understood? Don't you know that the LORD is the everlasting God, the Creator of all the earth? He never grows faint or weary. No one can measure the depths of his understanding.

James 1:5-7 warns that doubt inhibits prayer. When struggling with doubts, we should ask God to give us the gift of faith and then wait expectantly for his answer.

If you need wisdom—if you want to know what God wants you to do—ask him, and he will gladly tell you. He will not resent your asking. But when you ask him, be sure that you really expect him to answer, for a doubtful mind is as unsettled as a wave of the sea that is driven and tossed by the wind. People like that should not expect to receive anything from the Lord.

FOR FURTHER STUDY
- Doubts come when the focus is taken off Jesus (Matthew 14:31). *page 743*
- Doubt can make prayer ineffective (Matthew 21:21). *page 749*
- You should be considerate of the doubts of others (Romans 14:23). *page 877*
- Help those who have spiritual doubts (Hebrews 3:12). *page 935*

for EMOTIONAL HEALING

God created our emotions; we should turn to him for healing. Psalm 34:18 affirms God's love and care for those who need emotional healing.

The LORD is close to the brokenhearted; he rescues those who are crushed in spirit.

If you feel overwhelmed or caught in a hopeless situation, take heart. Acts 10:38 tells us that Jesus heals with power! Ask him to bring healing to your mind, spirit, and soul.

And no doubt you know that God anointed Jesus of Nazareth with the Holy Spirit and with power. Then Jesus went around doing good and healing all who were oppressed by the Devil, for God was with him.

FOR FURTHER STUDY
- Emotions can crush a person (Proverbs 15:13). *page 515*
- Do not be led by emotions (Proverbs 19:2). *page 517*
- Emotions are not reliable guides (Galatians 5:13-17). *pages 905-906*
- Some emotions can lead to sin (Ephesians 4:31). *page 909*

for ENCOURAGEMENT

In his darkest moments, the psalm writer turned to God for help. Psalm 42:8, 11 describes the encouragement the writer received from the Lord.

Through each day the LORD pours his unfailing love upon me, and through each night I sing his songs, praying to God who gives me life. Why am I discouraged? Why so sad? I will put my hope in God! I will praise him again—my Savior and my God!

Isaiah encouraged the Israelites to turn to God for help in their time of need. Isaiah 40:27-31 portrays the Lord as a shelter for the weary, a refuge for the weak.

O Israel, how can you say the LORD does not see your troubles? How can you say God refuses to hear your case? Have you never heard or understood? Don't you know that the LORD is the everlasting God, the Creator of all the earth? He never grows faint or weary. No one can measure the depths of his understanding. He gives power to those who are tired and worn out; he offers strength to the weak. Even youths will become exhausted, and young men will give up. But those who wait on the LORD will find new strength. They will fly high on wings like eagles. They will run and not grow weary. They will walk and not faint.

Romans 15:4 reveals one of the purposes of God's Word—to encourage God's people. Remembering what God has accomplished for his people in the past can give us new hope for the future.

Such things were written in the Scriptures long ago to teach us. They give us hope and encouragement as we wait patiently for God's promises.

An unsettling report from the doctor, a conflict at work, a lingering illness, a financial reversal, or a broken relationship—numerous setbacks and troubles can undermine our comfortable security and steal our dreams, causing us to be discouraged and sad and even to despair.

But focusing on our great God can encourage us and renew our strength. The wonderful truth is that the loving Father directs our ways and guides each of our steps during the day. And at night, when we sleep, he still stands with us, watching and protecting. When we turn our attention to God, discouragement transforms into hope and sorrow into praise.

What troubling questions, doubts, and struggles are dragging you down? Take your eyes off your circumstances and turn to your Lord—look up instead of down. Then you will gain new hope, knowing that you are secure in God's loving arms.

FOR FURTHER STUDY
- Good leaders should encourage followers to obey God (Numbers 13:30). *page 121*
- God's presence should encourage you (Joshua 1:1-9). *page 177*
- Encouragement comes from reading God's Word (Psalm 119:28). *page 493*
- Times of prayer bring encouragement (Psalm 138:3). *page 501*

- The Holy Spirit encourages you (Acts 9:31). *page 844*
- Your position in Christ encourages you (Philippians 2:1). *page 913*
- Believers should encourage each other (1 Thessalonians 4:18). *page 921*

for ENDURANCE

Paul asked God to give perseverance to his friends in Thessalonica. Likewise, we can pray for endurance for ourselves and others. Second Thessalonians 3:5 gives us the words to pray:

May the Lord bring you into an ever deeper understanding of the love of God and the endurance that comes from Christ.

The writer of the book of Hebrews encourages believers to persevere in their faith when they encounter troubles. If we endure, we will enjoy all of God's promises. Hebrews 10:36 says:

Patient endurance is what you need now, so you will continue to do God's will. Then you will receive all that he has promised.

Second Peter 1:6 explains the steps we can take to develop endurance—the first step is to seek to know God, and the end result is godliness.

Knowing God leads to self-control. Self-control leads to patient endurance, and patient endurance leads to godliness.

for EQUALITY

Galatians 3:28 teaches that all believers are equal in God's sight through Jesus Christ. You don't need to *fight* for equality—you already have it. Instead, work for unity.

> *There is no longer Jew or Gentile, slave or free, male or female. For you are all Christians—you are one in Christ Jesus.*

In Paul's day, Jews believed they were superior to Gentiles. But Paul declared in Ephesians 2:14 that the walls of prejudice could be broken through the power of Jesus. Because of Christ's sacrifice, *all* people, Jews and Gentiles alike, can experience reconciliation with God and each other. The same message is relevant today—we can look beyond

social and cultural barriers and enjoy equality and
unity with one another through Jesus Christ.

> *For Christ himself has made peace between us
> Jews and you Gentiles by making us all one
> people. He has broken down the wall of hostility
> that used to separate us.*

FOR FURTHER STUDY
- Women and men are both created in God's image (Genesis 1:26-28). *page 3*
- All believers have an equal share in God's inheritance (Ephesians 3:6). *page 908*
- Husbands and wives should be equal partners in marriage (1 Peter 3:7). *page 951*

for ETERNAL LIFE

At the tomb of his dear friend Lazarus, Jesus
assured Mary and Martha that he had power over
life and death. He declared in John 11:25:

> *"I am the resurrection and the life. Those who
> believe in me, even though they die like everyone
> else, will live again."*

God promises eternal life to those who follow
him. Paul affirms in Titus 1:2 that this is a promise we can count on.

> *This truth gives them the confidence of eternal
> life, which God promised them before the world
> began—and he cannot lie.*

When Jesus spoke with the Samaritan woman at the well, he offered her eternal life. Relating his offer to physical thirst, he described *his* water as a perpetual spring, quenching thirst forever. His words are recorded in John 4:13-14:

> *Jesus replied, "People soon become thirsty again after drinking this water. But the water I give them takes away thirst altogether. It becomes a perpetual spring within them, giving them eternal life."*

Jesus could promise eternal life because he was God in the flesh—the author of life and the giver of eternal life. And when Jesus makes a promise, we can be sure that he will fulfill it—all those who drink *will* live forever.

Are you frustrated with this world, its pain and struggles? Remember, this life is not all there is.

Are you thirsty for meaning, purpose, and significance? Remember, water from Jesus will quench your longings and deepest needs.

Have you visited numerous "wells" in your search? Remember, Jesus alone is the source of this eternal spring!

FOR FURTHER STUDY
- Eternal life is only for those who do God's will (Matthew 7:21). *page 735*
- The righteous will receive eternal life (Matthew 25:46). *page 754*
- Belief in Jesus is required for eternal life (John 3:15-16). *page 814*
- Evil people will receive eternal punishment (John 5:28-29). *page 816*
- Jesus came to give life (John 10:10). *page 823*
- Jesus is eternal life (John 14:6). *page 827*
- Eternal life cannot be earned (Ephesians 2:8-9). *page 908*
- Eternal life gives hope (Titus 3:7). *page 932*

for ETERNAL REWARDS

Ruth, a Moabite widow, demonstrated great faith in the God of Israel. Boaz, a relative of Ruth's mother-in-law, was impressed by Ruth's faithfulness and diligence. He assured her that God would reward her for her consistent obedience to him. Ruth 2:10-12 says:

> Ruth fell at his feet and thanked him warmly. "Why are you being so kind to me?" she asked. "I am only a foreigner." "Yes, I know," Boaz replied. "But I also know about the love and kindness you have shown your mother-in-law since the death of your husband. I have heard how you left your father and mother and your own land to live here among complete strangers. May the LORD, the God of Israel, under whose wings you have come to take refuge, reward you fully."

When David saw unjust people succeeding, he cried out to God. In Psalm 58:11, David affirmed the fact that God would have the last word—God would judge the wicked and *reward* the righteous. We may not receive what is fair in this life, but we can know that God will reward us in the next life.

> Then at last everyone will say, "There truly is a reward for those who live for God; surely there is a God who judges justly here on earth."

Luke 6:35 explains that we can store up rewards in heaven by obeying God and loving our enemies.

> *[Jesus said] "Love your enemies! Do good to them! Lend to them! And don't be concerned that they might not repay. Then your reward from heaven will be very great, and you will truly be acting as children of the Most High, for he is kind to the unthankful and to those who are wicked."*

FOR FURTHER STUDY

- God rewards those who obey him faithfully (1 Samuel 25:28). *page 242*
- God rewards you with his unfailing love (2 Samuel 2:6). *page 248*
- The reward God gives will last forever (Psalm 37:18). *page 449*
- You will receive your reward when Christ returns (Isaiah 40:10). *page 561*
- Obeying God yields great rewards in his Kingdom (Matthew 5:19). *page 732*
- God rewards those who seek him (Hebrews 11:6). *page 941*

to overcome EVIL

David knew he was prone to sin, so he prayed in Psalm 19:13 that God would help him guard against evil. We can follow his example and ask God to make us strong in resisting evil.

Keep me from deliberate sins! Don't let them control me. Then I will be free of guilt and innocent of great sin.

Having Jesus in our lives should make a real difference in the way we respond to temptation. His Spirit empowers us to resist sin and be transformed in our thoughts and actions. Ephesians 4:21-24 highlights the importance of depending on Jesus to resist evil.

Since you have heard all about him and have learned the truth that is in Jesus, throw off your old evil nature and your former way of life, which is rotten through and through, full of lust and deception. Instead, there must be a spiritual renewal of your thoughts and attitudes. You must display a new nature because you are a new person, created in God's likeness—righteous, holy, and true.

FOR FURTHER STUDY
- Believers should refuse to join in with evil (Psalm 26:5). *page 443*
- God allows people to choose evil (Romans 1:24-28). *pages 865-866*
- God cannot coexist with evil (Galatians 5:16-17). *page 906*
- There are spiritual forces behind evil (Ephesians 6:12). *page 911*

for help in dealing with FAILURE

David had committed adultery and murder and then had lied about it—his failure was serious and the consequences far-reaching. In Psalm 51:2-4, he admitted his failure to God and asked for forgiveness.

Wash me clean from my guilt. Purify me from my sin. For I recognize my shameful deeds—they haunt me day and night Against you, and you alone, have I sinned; I have done what is evil in your sight. You will be proved right in what you say, and your judgment against me is just.

Ecclesiastes 10:4 reveals that the best way to deal with your failures is to humbly learn from them and move on.

A quiet spirit can overcome even great mistakes.

It's easy to judge others for their mistakes, but we should try to learn from them instead. Isaiah 42:23 instructs us to avoid failure by learning from other people's mistakes.

Will not even one of you apply these lessons from the past and see the ruin that awaits you?

FOR FURTHER STUDY
- Admit your failures quickly and try to make amends (Genesis 41:9). *page 35*
- Try to learn from your failures (Leviticus 26:23-24). *page 106*

- The fear of failure causes people to hide (1 Samuel 10:22). *page 228*
- Controlling your tongue can help you avoid failure (James 3:2). *page 946*

for FAITH

Abram had demonstrated his faith in God through his actions, but Genesis 15:6 makes it clear that it was his belief, not his actions, that made him right with God.

And Abram believed the LORD, and the LORD declared him righteous because of his faith.

Hebrews 11:1 defines faith—it is believing God will fulfill his promises before we see any proof or evidence of it.

What is faith? It is the confident assurance that what we hope for is going to happen. It is the evidence of things we cannot yet see.

Job was a man who suffered greatly, more than anyone can ever imagine. Yet, in the midst of unbearable pain, he affirmed his faith in God. Job 19:25-27 is an amazing declaration of Job's faith.

"But as for me, I know that my Redeemer lives, and that he will stand upon the earth at last. And after my body has decayed, yet in my body I will see God! I will see him for myself. Yes, I will see him with my own eyes. I am overwhelmed at the thought!"

Consider Job's condition. He had lost all his children, livestock, and possessions. Everything had been taken except his wife, who had reacted by telling him to "curse God and die" (Job 2:9). Next, he had become afflicted with boils. Then his friends showed up and, after a time of silence, began to recite mindless counsel and accusations of unnamed sins. What devastating pain and loneliness! The natural reaction would have been to become embittered and take his wife's advice.

But Job's faith was rooted in God—not in his situation or surroundings. He knew that his Redeemer was alive and in control. Despite Job's terrible physical and emotional pain, he could look beyond his circumstances to the Lord and beyond his present condition to the future.

Few, if any, have suffered as much as Job did. Few, if any, have expressed such deep faith.

What pain do you endure? Learn with Job that God can meet you in your need. Put your faith in God! As Holocaust survivor Corrie ten Boom stated, "No matter how deep the pit, God is deeper still."

FOR FURTHER STUDY
- Even a small amount of faith can do great things (Luke 17:6). *page 802*
- Individuals are made right with God through faith (Romans 3:28). *page 867*
- Faith puts you in a right relationship with God (Romans 5:1). *page 868*
- Faith comes from hearing the Word of God (Romans 10:17). *page 873*
- Accept the person who has weak faith (Romans 14:1). *page 876*

• Faith accompanies obedience to God (Hebrews 11:7-12).
  page 941

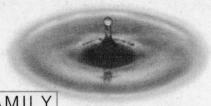

for FAMILY

In his great love, God has adopted us as his children. Ephesians 1:5 confirms this wonderful truth! When our earthly family disappoints us, we can gain comfort and hope from the fact that we are part of the family of God.

His unchanging plan has always been to adopt us into his own family by bringing us to himself through Jesus Christ. And this gave him great pleasure.

Ephesians 2:19 tells believers that they belong to God's family. The bond we have with fellow believers can be stronger than natural family ties.

So now you Gentiles are no longer strangers and foreigners. You are citizens along with all of God's holy people. You are members of God's family.

FOR FURTHER STUDY
• Your earthly family will not meet all your needs (Psalm 38:11). *page 450*
• Integrity in a home honors God (Psalm 101:2). *page 482*
• One family member can bring grief to the whole family (Proverbs 15:27). *page 515*
• True faith is of greater importance than family (Luke 12:51-53). *page 798*

- Families should take care of each other (1 Timothy 5:3-4). *page 926*
- Through Christ, you are a member of God's family (1 John 3:1-3). *page 957*

to overcome FEAR

Knowing he would soon leave his disciples, Jesus offered them words of encouragement and comfort. He promised that the Spirit of God would bring them peace that could overcome all of their fears. John 14:27 records his promise:

> *"I am leaving you with a gift—peace of mind and heart. And the peace I give isn't like the peace the world gives. So don't be troubled or afraid."*

First John 4:18 tells us to focus on God's great love when we are afraid—his love has the power to calm our fears.

> *Such love has no fear because perfect love expels all fear. If we are afraid, it is for fear of judgment, and this shows that his love has not been perfected in us.*

Hebrews 2:14-15 teaches us that Christ broke the power of death through his death and resurrection. As a result, we do not need to fear death any longer—Christ has conquered it.

> *Because God's children are human beings—made of flesh and blood—Jesus also became flesh and*

63

blood by being born in human form. For only as a human being could he die, and only by dying could he break the power of the Devil, who had the power of death. Only in this way could he deliver those who have lived all their lives as slaves to the fear of dying.

Fear paralyzes, especially the fear of death.

Fearing for their safety, some people scarcely venture out into the world. They become imprisoned in their own homes. While most do not live at that extreme, nearly everyone, if honest, would admit to fearing death. It's always there, lurking beneath the surface. That's what motivates many to exercise endlessly and to consume large quantities of vitamins—trying, almost desperately, to postpone the inevitable.

The truth, however, is that with each passing day our flesh and bones lose their youthful beauty and vigor, bringing us face-to-face with our own mortality. The reality of death can be frustrating and frightening.

Those who follow Christ also die, but they don't die forever. They live again through the power of their risen and triumphant Lord. When Jesus died on the cross, he took the death penalty for all who trust in him. When Jesus rose from the grave, he conquered that fearful enemy. And his resurrection holds the promise that we also will rise.

Don't be enslaved to fear. Christ has set you free by destroying the power of death. Live with the joyful knowledge that you have eternal life.

FOR FURTHER STUDY
• God will not forget you (Genesis 46:3). *page 40*
• You should fear God (Psalm 25:12). *page 442*

for FORGIVENESS

The psalm writer rejoiced in the fact that God forgives the sins of his people. Psalm 65:3 states:

Though our hearts are filled with sins, you forgive them all.

If you doubt God's forgiveness, allow the words of Romans 8:32 to strengthen your faith. If God gave up his only Son for you, so surely he will not hold back his forgiveness!

Since God did not spare even his own Son but gave him up for us all, won't God, who gave us Christ, also give us everything else?

God's forgiveness is different than human forgiveness. Isaiah 43:25 declares that when God forgives sins, he forgets them forever.

"I—yes, I alone—am the one who blots out your sins for my own sake and will never think of them again."

Human forgiveness often comes with hidden strings. We say we forgive, but later, at a crucial time, we yank the string and pull the offense back into view. Saying "I forgive you" comes easily, but truly forgiving and *forgetting* is much more difficult. Perhaps that's why we struggle with guilt, even after we have asked God to forgive. Knowing our tendency to store past offenses and hold grudges, we assume that God does the same.

But the Bible proclaims that God will never think of our sins again. Does God take sin seriously? Definitely! Sin is so serious that it deserves the death penalty, eternal death.

Does God *want* to forgive sinners? Certainly! God sent Jesus to take the punishment for sin, dying on the cross in our place. All who repent and trust in Christ can be forgiven.

Can we trust God to forgive us? Of course!

Release that load of guilt. Stand tall and breathe the sweet air of forgiveness.

FOR FURTHER STUDY
- God forgives you because he loves you (Psalm 86:5).
  page 475
- God washes you as clean as fresh snow (Isaiah 1:18).
  page 537
- God removes your impurities (Ezekiel 36:25). *page 657*
- God loves to forgive (Micah 7:18). *page 706*
- God's children are reborn spiritually (John 1:12-13). *page 812*
- Christians should be free from sin's power (Romans 5:21).
  page 869
- God will forgive your sins if you confess (1 John 1:8-9).
  page 956

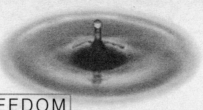

for FREEDOM

Some people expect that obeying God will limit or restrain them, but Psalm 119:45 reveals that true freedom comes through living God's way. He knows what is best for us!

I will walk in freedom, for I have devoted myself to your commandments.

Jesus claims in John 8:31-32 that the truth can set us free. How? God's truth sets us free from the ravages of sin, from self-delusion, and from deception. Sin enslaves, but Jesus is the truth that sets us free.

Jesus said to the people who believed in him, "You are truly my disciples if you keep obeying my teachings. And you will know the truth, and the truth will set you free."

The more you devote yourself to God, the more freedom you will find. Galatians 5:13 describes the freedom God gives:

For you have been called to live in freedom—not freedom to satisfy your sinful nature, but freedom to serve one another in love.

FOR FURTHER STUDY
- Freedom is found in obeying God (Genesis 3:4-5).
  page 4
- Salvation is freedom from sin and death (Psalm 68:19-21).
  page 464

- Christians are spiritually free (John 8:36). *page 821*
- Christians are free from sin's power (Romans 5:21). *page 869*
- Being a slave to Christ brings freedom (1 Corinthians 7:23). *page 883*

for FRIENDSHIP

Sometimes it is difficult to know who your real friends are. Proverbs 17:17 describes qualities of a true friend, the kind on whom you can depend.

A friend is always loyal, and a brother is born to help in time of need.

Jesus modeled true friendship for his followers— he willingly laid down his life for his friends. In John 15:12-13, he instructed his disciples to do the same.

"I command you to love each other in the same way that I love you. And here is how to measure it—the greatest love is shown when people lay down their lives for their friends."

The wisest man who ever lived knew the importance of friendship. In Ecclesiastes 4:9-10 and 12, Solomon described the benefits of having friends.

Two people can accomplish more than twice as much as one; they get a better return for their labor. If one person falls, the other can reach out and help. But people who are alone when they fall are in real trouble. A person standing alone can be attacked and defeated, but two can stand back-to-back and conquer. Three are even better, for a triple-braided cord is not easily broken.

Friends work together, help each other, defend one another, and encourage each other. In contrast, the person without any friends must face the world alone. We need friends to encourage and support us, to give feedback and hold us accountable, to console and counsel us, and to direct us to God.

At times, we may feel as though we would rather go it alone; after all, friendships require maintenance, and that means work. But God has created us as relational beings (Genesis 2:18), and he wants us to share his love with others, not to keep it to ourselves (1 Corinthians 13). And he promises to be our friend, one who "sticks closer than a brother" (Proverbs 18:24).

Friends are gifts from God. Receive his gifts with gratitude. And be a gift to someone who needs a friend.

FOR FURTHER STUDY
- A good friend is a blessing from God (1 Samuel 18:3-4). *page 236*
- A true friend remains faithful through good times and bad (Proverbs 18:24). *page 517*
- Friends have a strong influence (Proverbs 22:24-25). *page 519*
- Friendships should not compromise your faith (2 Corinthians 6:14-18). *page 896*

for the FRUIT OF THE SPIRIT

Jesus described himself as the vine and God as the gardener who prunes the branches (believers) to make them fruitful. John 15:5 assures us that when we are joined with the vine, we will produce much fruit.

"Yes, I am the vine; you are the branches. Those who remain in me, and I in them, will produce much fruit. For apart from me you can do nothing."

If we love and obey God, he *will* produce the fruits of his Spirit in our lives. Galatians 5:22-23 lists the fruit God wants to develop in us:

But when the Holy Spirit controls our lives, he will produce this kind of fruit in us: love, joy, peace, patience, kindness, goodness, faithfulness, gentleness, and self-control. Here there is no conflict with the law.

When we allow God's Spirit to produce fruit in our lives, God is glorified. We can use Paul's prayer in Philippians 1:11 to ask God to produce fruit in us for his glory.

May you always be filled with the fruit of your salvation—those good things that are produced in your life by Jesus Christ—for this will bring much glory and praise to God.

FOR FURTHER STUDY
- Lack of fruitfulness will be judged (Matthew 3:10). *page 731*
- Jesus made an example of fruitlessness (Matthew 21:19). *page 749*
- Christians should be faithful to bear fruit (Matthew 25:29-30). *page 754*
- God prunes away unfruitfulness (John 15:1-4). *page 828*

for FULFILLMENT

David was filled with loneliness while hiding in the desert from his enemies. He found great comfort and fulfillment in meditating on God and his faithfulness. He declared in Psalm 63:2-5 that God could fulfill his needs better than anyone or anything.

I have seen you in your sanctuary and gazed upon your power and glory. Your unfailing love is better to me than life itself; how I praise you! I will honor you as long as I live, lifting up my hands to you in prayer. You satisfy me more than the richest of foods. I will praise you with songs of joy.

Many people believe material things will make them happy. But the Bible says that true fulfillment comes to those who seek God. Jesus tells us in Matthew 6:31-34 that only God can satisfy our deepest desires.

"So don't worry about having enough food or drink or clothing. Why be like the pagans who are

so deeply concerned about these things? Your heavenly Father already knows all your needs, and he will give you all you need from day to day if you live for him and make the Kingdom of God your primary concern. So don't worry about tomorrow, for tomorrow will bring its own worries. Today's trouble is enough for today."

FOR FURTHER STUDY
- Fulfillment from earthly things is impossible (Ecclesiastes 1:8-11). *page 526*
- God offers true spiritual fulfillment (Isaiah 55:1-13). *page 571*
- There is danger in feeling too satisfied (Hosea 13:6). *page 690*
- True fulfillment is found in God's Kingdom (Matthew 13:44-46). *page 742*
- Only God can satisfy spiritual thirst (John 4:13-14). *page 815*

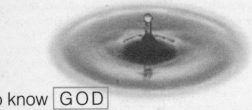

to know GOD

The psalm writer acknowledged in Psalm 42:1-2 that we are all made with an emptiness that only God can fill.

As the deer pants for streams of water, so I long for you, O God. I thirst for God, the living God. When can I come and stand before him?

Abraham discovered the secret to knowing God. He was called a "friend of God" because of his *faith.* James 2:23 reveals that we also can find friendship with God through faith.

> *And so it happened just as the Scriptures say: "Abraham believed God, so God declared him to be righteous." He was even called "the friend of God."*

The Bible tells us that if we seek God, he will reveal himself to us. James 4:8 promises:

> *Draw close to God, and God will draw close to you.*

FOR FURTHER STUDY

- God is trustworthy (Deuteronomy 7:9). *page 152*
- God is gracious and merciful (Nehemiah 9:31). *page 400*
- God is your hope (Psalm 71:5). *page 466*
- God is always near (Psalm 75:1). *pages 468-469*
- God is the Father of every believer (Matthew 6:9). *page 733*
- God is spirit (John 4:24). *page 815*
- God is knowable (Ephesians 1:17). *page 907*

to see GOD AT WORK

If you humbly ask God's Spirit to open your eyes, you will see God at work all around you. Psalm 69:32 promises,

> *The humble will see their God at work and be glad. Let all who seek God's help live in joy.*

God reveals his plans to us by his Holy Spirit. First Corinthians 2:10 teaches we can ask God to reveal himself and his work to us.

But we know these things because God has revealed them to us by his Spirit, and his Spirit searches out everything and shows us even God's deep secrets.

FOR FURTHER STUDY

- All of God's work is good (Genesis 1:31). *page 3*
- God's work is perfect (Deuteronomy 32:4). *page 172*
- God is at work, even if you can't see it (Judges 14:4). *page 211*
- God's work is bigger and greater than anyone can know (Ecclesiastes 3:11). *page 527*
- Strive to be part of God's work (1 Corinthians 7:30). *page 883*

for GOD'S KINGDOM

In Matthew 13:44, Jesus compared God's Kingdom to hidden treasure. His Kingdom is more valuable than life itself and entering it requires self-sacrifice.

"The Kingdom of Heaven is like a treasure that a man discovered hidden in a field. In his excitement, he hid it again and sold everything he owned to get enough money to buy the field—and to get the treasure, too!"

When Jesus' disciples began arguing about which of them would be the greatest in God's Kingdom, Jesus used a child to teach them a lesson. We learn from Jesus' words in Matthew 18:2-3 that God grants entrance into his Kingdom only to those people who humbly admit their weaknesses and depend wholly on God.

> *Jesus called a small child over to him and put the child among them. Then he said, "I assure you, unless you turn from your sins and become as little children, you will never get into the Kingdom of Heaven."*

Jesus declares the simple truth of the gospel in John 3:3. Humility, repentance, and faith in God are all we need to become part of God's Kingdom.

> *Jesus replied, "I assure you, unless you are born again, you can never see the Kingdom of God."*

FOR FURTHER STUDY
- Legalism will not help us enter God's Kingdom (Matthew 5:20). *page 732*
- God's Kingdom is open to those who do his will (Matthew 7:21). *page 735*
- God's Kingdom is within people's hearts (Luke 17:20-21). *page 802*
- God's Kingdom will fully arrive in the future (Luke 21:25-31). *page 807*
- Entering God's Kingdom is not easy (Acts 14:22). *pages 849-850*
- God's Kingdom is powerful (1 Corinthians 4:20). *page 881*
- God calls people into his Kingdom (1 Thessalonians 2:12). *page 919*
- God's Kingdom will one day be fully established (Revelation 11:15). *page 970*

for GOD'S PRESENCE

David rejoiced in God's presence. Psalm 68:3 encourages us to do the same.

> *But let the godly rejoice. Let them be glad in God's presence. Let them be filled with joy.*

Ephesians 3:12 teaches that we can enter God's presence with confidence because of the work of Jesus Christ. In fact, we can *believe* in God's presence even when we don't *feel* it.

> *Because of Christ and our faith in him, we can now come fearlessly into God's presence, assured of his glad welcome.*

FOR FURTHER STUDY
- Pride and God's presence are incompatible (Psalm 10:11). *page 435*
- God's presence is all you need (Psalm 27:4). *page 443*
- God's presence helps you through problems (Psalm 34:18-19). *page 447*
- We cannot hide from God's presence (Psalm 140:12). *page 502*

to know GOD'S WILL

God wants you to do his will—ask him for help and he will give you wisdom to know what to do and courage to obey. James 1:5 offers this promise to you:

> *If you need wisdom—if you want to know what God wants you to do—ask him, and he will gladly tell you. He will not resent your asking.*

God has revealed much of his will to us through the Bible. Hebrews 10:36 encourages you to patiently obey what you already know is right and God will bless you.

> *Patient endurance is what you need now, so you will continue to do God's will. Then you will receive all that he has promised.*

God's Word is the perfect place to look for guidance from the Lord. Psalm 19:7-8 reminds us of the value of the Scriptures:

> *The law of the LORD is perfect, reviving the soul. The decrees of the LORD are trustworthy, making wise the simple. The commandments of the LORD are right, bringing joy to the heart. The commands of the LORD are clear, giving insight to life.*

Do you want to know God's will? Read his book.
  Do you want to know how to please God? Read the Scriptures.

Do you want to know how to live? Read God's Word.

Check out God's law, statutes, precepts, commands, and ordinances. They are "perfect," "trustworthy," "right," "clear," and "pure." And following them will bring revival, wisdom, joy, and insight!

Don't lose your way in the fog of worldly values and human understanding. Study God's message, learn his truths, and follow his instruction; then you will know his will for you. He will help you stay on the right road and move in the right direction.

FOR FURTHER STUDY
- God guides you (Psalm 16:7). *page 437*
- Ask God for guidance (Psalm 25:4-7). *page 442*
- God will direct you (Psalm 48:14). *page 455*
- God directs the plans that you commit to him (Proverbs 16:3). *page 515*
- God works everything out according to his plan (Proverbs 16:4). *page 515*
- God directs events (Acts 16:6-7). *page 851*

for GOODNESS

God's power and goodness are so great that he can use the bad things in our lives and turn them around for good. Joseph, who was betrayed by his brothers and sold into slavery, declared God's goodness to him in Genesis 50:20. God used the evil actions of Joseph's brothers to bring good into Joseph's life for the benefit of his whole family.

> *As far as I am concerned, God turned into good what you meant for evil. He brought me to the high position I have today so I could save the lives of many people.*

Psalm 31:19 boldly declares the goodness of the Lord. God's goodness is all around us—we should praise him for it!

> *Your goodness is so great! You have stored up great blessings for those who honor you. You have done so much for those who come to you for protection, blessing them before the watching world.*

Do you believe that God is *completely* good? When you have doubts or fears, read Psalm 92:15. The psalm writer reminds us that God is filled with goodness—we can trust him completely with every aspect of our lives.

> *They will declare, "The LORD is just! He is my rock! There is nothing but goodness in him!"*

FOR FURTHER STUDY
- God can bring goodness from bad circumstances (Genesis 16:13). *page 13*
- God is eager to give his children good gifts (Matthew 7:9-11). *page 734*
- Goodness alone won't guarantee eternal life (Matthew 7:21-23). *page 735*
- We must depend on the Lord in order to produce good things (John 15:5-8). *page 828*
- God works all things for good (Romans 8:28). *page 871*

to share the GOSPEL

The Holy Spirit will give you power, courage, and wisdom to share the gospel. In Acts 1:8, Jesus promises:

> *"But when the Holy Spirit has come upon you, you will receive power and will tell people about me everywhere—in Jerusalem, throughout Judea, in Samaria, and to the ends of the earth."*

The only way the early church could grow was through believers preaching the gospel. Paul encouraged Timothy in 2 Timothy 4:2 to be ready at all times to share the word of God with others, whether it was convenient or not. We should do the same.

> *Preach the word of God. Be persistent, whether the time is favorable or not. Patiently correct, rebuke, and encourage your people with good teaching.*

FOR FURTHER STUDY

- You are God's messenger (Isaiah 43:10-11). *page 564*
- Christians bring light to a spiritually dark world (Matthew 5:14-16). *page 732*
- Do not be ashamed to be a Christian (Matthew 10:33). *page 738*
- The gospel's message is for everyone (Luke 24:46-47). *page 811*

- People should respond to the gospel with faith (John 1:12). *page 812*
- The gospel is powerful (Romans 1:16). *page 865*
- Believing the gospel brings a change to life (1 Thessalonians 1:4-5). *page 919*

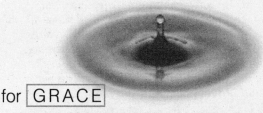

for GRACE

Paul knew that he faced prison and suffering and that he might not see his close friends in Ephesus again. Instead of worrying about them, however, he trusted that God's grace would protect them. In Acts 20:32, he says:

"And now I entrust you to God and the word of his grace—his message that is able to build you up and give you an inheritance with all those he has set apart for himself."

Paul had been an enemy of the Christian church until God saved him. He freely acknowledged in 1 Corinthians 15:10 that he had accomplished much for Christ only because of God's grace working through him.

But whatever I am now, it is all because God poured out his special favor on me—and not without results. For I have worked harder than all the other apostles, yet it was not I but God who was working through me by his grace.

First Corinthians was a difficult letter for Paul to write because the Corinthian church was struggling with conflict and division. Yet Paul affirmed God's work for and in the believers there. In 1 Corinthians 1:7-9, he reminded them that God's grace would keep them strong.

> *Now you have every spiritual gift you need as you eagerly wait for the return of our Lord Jesus Christ. He will keep you strong right up to the end, and he will keep you free from all blame on the great day when our Lord Jesus Christ returns. God will surely do this for you, for he always does just what he says, and he is the one who invited you into this wonderful friendship with his Son, Jesus Christ our Lord.*

The Bible teaches us that the Christian life depends totally on God. He calls, gives faith, saves by faith, confirms salvation, distributes spiritual gifts, strengthens, and keeps till the end.

God's favor is undeserved. No one can earn it—not in the first century and not today, neither the Corinthians nor you. That's God's faithful grace!

Regardless of your past sins or present condition, if you have trusted in Christ as Savior, God's grace is working in you. His plan is to conform you to the image of Christ, to present you "free from all blame on the great day when our Lord Jesus Christ returns." So stop struggling. Receive his grace and allow him to continue his good work in your life.

FOR FURTHER STUDY
- God is full of grace (Exodus 34:6). *page 75*
- Grace is a good gift from the Lord (Psalm 84:11). *page 475*
- God's provision is an expression of his grace (Joel 2:23). *page 692*
- God's grace gives you power to obey him (Acts 6:8). *page 840*

- God's grace helps you remain faithful (Acts 13:43). *page 849*
- God's grace frees you from sin (Romans 6:14). *page 869*
- Depend on God's grace, not your own wisdom (2 Corinthians 1:12). *page 893*
- God's grace makes salvation possible (Ephesians 1:7-8). *page 907*
- God accepts you by his grace (Ephesians 2:8-9). *page 908*
- God's grace gives hope (1 Peter 1:13). *page 949*

for GREATNESS

Jesus turned the world's values upside down. While most people strive for attention, power, and status, Jesus encouraged his followers to do the opposite. In Matthew 20:16, Jesus advises us to be content working behind the scenes, to serve others with humility, if we want to be great in God's Kingdom.

"And so it is, that many who are first now will be last then; and those who are last now will be first then."

God's view of greatness is different than the world's perspective. Jesus tells us in Luke 9:48 that those who humble themselves and seek to serve others will achieve greatness in God's eyes.

Then [Jesus] said to them, "Anyone who welcomes a little child like this on my behalf welcomes me, and anyone who welcomes me welcomes my

Father who sent me. Whoever is the least among you is the greatest."

FOR FURTHER STUDY
- God often defeats the plans of those who seek personal greatness (Genesis 11:3-8). *page 9*
- Jesus describes those who are great in God's Kingdom (Matthew 5:3-12). *page 732*
- The greatest in God's Kingdom are as humble as children (Matthew 18:1-10). *page 746*
- Greatness is gained through service (Matthew 20:20-27). *page 748*
- A humble act of sacrifice proves greatness (Mark 14:1-9). *page 775*

for help in dealing with GRIEF

David's words in Psalm 23 have brought comfort to countless people. They remind us that God is our comfort and protection, even in our darkest moments of grief. Psalm 23:4 says:

Even when I walk through the dark valley of death, I will not be afraid, for you are close beside me. Your rod and your staff protect and comfort me.

When we are filled with grief, God's Word can bring us comfort and strength. In Psalm 119:28, the psalm writer acknowledges his need for God and his belief in God's goodness.

I weep with grief; encourage me by your word.

Jesus knew his disciples would experience loss and persecution because of their faith in him. In anticipation of those difficulties, Jesus promised God's comfort and blessing to those who mourn. Matthew 5:4 says:

> *God blesses those who mourn, for they will be comforted.*

Why? We silently shout to God as we stand by the grave of a loved one. Overwhelmed by grief, we question God's goodness and wonder how he could allow such suffering and pain. Death seems such a defeat. And that's not all: Each day brings a multitude of reasons for discouragement and despair—lost dreams, broken promises, hurt feelings, persecution, misunderstanding, disease, war, natural disaster. . . .

Yet Jesus could say that those who mourn will be blessed. And don't forget that Jesus would experience the death of a close friend, rejection by family and friends, physical and verbal abuse from religious leaders, disappointment with inconsistent disciples, betrayal by a close associate, and, ultimately, an excruciating death on the cross.

Jesus knew that this life is not all there is and that those who trust in him will find deep comfort, profound peace, and unending joy in his presence.

Whatever the cause, let your grief push you toward the Savior. You will be comforted.

FOR FURTHER STUDY
• Grief is often a necessary part of repentance (Judges 2:4-5). *page 199*

- God comforts you in your darkest times (Job 35:10). *page 428*
- Weeping will be followed by joy (Psalm 30:5). *page 444*
- God desires to comfort and restore his people (Isaiah 40:1-31). *pages 561-562*
- Jesus understands sorrow (Isaiah 53:3-9). *page 570*
- The Holy Spirit comforts you (Acts 9:31). *page 844*
- The Bible tells us about God's comforting promises (Romans 15:4). *page 877*
- We can pass along to others the comfort God has given us (2 Corinthians 1:3-11). *page 893*
- God may use sorrow to draw people back to him (2 Corinthians 7:10-11). *page 897*

for GUIDANCE

David praised God in Psalm 16:7 for giving him the insight and instruction he needed to follow God's way.

I will bless the LORD who guides me; even at night my heart instructs me.

God is eager to guide us, but our stubbornness can get in the way. Psalm 32:8-9 tells us that if we want to be used by God, we need to let him guide us one step at a time.

The LORD says, "I will guide you along the best pathway for your life. I will advise you and watch over you. Do not be like a senseless horse or mule that needs a bit and bridle to keep it under control."

Instead of trying to control and manage our lives, God wants us to trust and depend on him. If we will give God control, he promises in Proverbs 3:5-6 to guide us.

Trust in the LORD with all your heart; do not depend on your own understanding. Seek his will in all you do, and he will direct your paths.

The older we get, the more we realize how little knowledge we possess. We find we have more and more questions and fewer and fewer answers. Instead of being black and white, life seems filled with gray areas. We struggle with complex issues and problems that have no obvious solutions. We wonder what to do, which way to turn, how to live, and where to go. And we doubt.

God's promises give us hope. Note that God's Word doesn't offer simple solutions and easy answers; he offers himself. God says he will *guide*, *advise*, and *watch*. In other words, God will help us go in the right direction and then protect us on the road.

That's great news to finite, confused, and doubting human beings because it comes from the infinite, all-knowing, and all-powerful creator and ruler of the universe.

What life issues boggle your mind? What decisions slow you down? What problems harass your steps? Look to the Lord for guidance. He won't zap you to your destination, but he will guide you along the way.

FOR FURTHER STUDY
- Ask God for guidance (Psalm 25:4-7). *page 442*
- God will give direction (Psalm 48:14). *page 455*
- The Bible gives guidance (Psalm 119:133). *page 495*

- God works everything according to his plan (Proverbs 16:4). *page 515*
- God directs the events of your life (Acts 16:6-7). *page 851*
- God gives wisdom for making decisions (James 1:5). *page 945*

for freedom from GUILT

When we confess our sins, we should *believe* that God forgives us and *release* our sense of guilt. We are clean in God's eyes! The psalmist gives us a good example to follow in Psalm 32:5:

Finally, I confessed all my sins to you and stopped trying to hide them. I said to myself, "I will confess my rebellion to the LORD." And you forgave me! All my guilt is gone.

While in Pisidian Antioch, Paul and his companions entered the synagogue and were asked by the leaders to speak to the people. Paul boldly presented the gospel which is summarized in Acts 13:39—anyone who believes is Jesus will receive forgiveness and freedom from guilt.

Everyone who believes in him is freed from all guilt and declared right with God—something the Jewish law could never do.

Romans 3:23-24 explains that we can find freedom from guilt only through Jesus Christ. His death on the cross bridges the gap between a holy God and sinful people. We all have sinned, but Christ has paid the penalty for us and gives us freedom.

For all have sinned; all fall short of God's glorious standard. Yet now God in his gracious kindness declares us not guilty. He has done this through Christ Jesus, who has freed us by taking away our sins.

FOR FURTHER STUDY
- Guilt causes people to hide from God (Genesis 3:7-11). *page 4*
- Ask God to forgive hidden sins (Psalm 19:12-13). *page 440*
- God can cleanse you from all sin (Psalm 51:2). *page 456*
- God waits for people to admit their guilt (Hosea 5:15). *page 686*
- All people are guilty of sin (Romans 3:9-12). *page 867*

for HAPPINESS

Psalm 112:1-3 speaks of the many benefits of having faith in God. Happiness is one advantage of the Christian life. God also blesses his people with success, fulfillment, joy, and the hope of eternity with him.

Happy are those who fear the LORD. Yes, happy are those who delight in doing what he commands. Their children will be successful everywhere; an entire generation of godly people will be blessed. They themselves will be wealthy, and their good deeds will never be forgotten.

Proverbs 11:23 reveals the secret of happiness—
we will find it if we fear and honor God.

*The godly can look forward to happiness, while the
wicked can expect only wrath.*

Solomon wrote in Ecclesiastes 5:10 that those
who seek happiness by accumulating wealth will
never be satisfied. Happiness comes to those who
obey God.

*Those who love money will never have enough.
How absurd to think that wealth brings true
happiness!*

FOR FURTHER STUDY
- Obeying God brings happiness (Psalm 119:2). *page 492*
- Jesus describes happiness that can be found despite
  earthly troubles (Matthew 5:3-10). *page 732*
- The Holy Spirit produces joy (Galatians 5:22). *page 906*
- Happiness should not depend on circumstances
  (Philippians 4:4-12). *page 914*
- Sometimes happiness comes through pain (Hebrews 12:2).
  page 942
- Hard times can be an opportunity for joy (James 1:2). *page
  945*

for HEAVEN

The Pharisees of Jesus' day were meticulous in
their attempts to obey God's law, in addition to
all of the rules they had added to it. Yet, Jesus
claimed that a person must do a better job of

obedience than the Pharisees to enter the Kingdom of Heaven! In Matthew 5:20, Jesus was emphasizing the importance of heart condition, attitudes, and motives. We will gain entrance into heaven if we allow God to change us from the inside out.

> *"But I warn you—unless you obey God better than the teachers of religious law and the Pharisees do, you can't enter the Kingdom of Heaven at all!"*

Jesus is preparing a wonderful place to spend eternity with his followers. His promise in John 14:2-3 should make us look forward to going home to heaven!

> *"There are many rooms in my Father's home, and I am going to prepare a place for you. If this were not so, I would tell you plainly. When everything is ready, I will come and get you, so that you will always be with me where I am."*

Although we can feel comfortable and reasonably happy here, we must remember that earth is our temporary home—we're passing through on our way to a much better place. Paul encourages us in Colossians 3:1-4 to focus our thoughts and desires on eternal things to maintain a proper perspective.

> *Since you have been raised to new life with Christ, set your sights on the realities of heaven, where Christ sits at God's right hand in the place of honor and power. Let heaven fill your thoughts. Do not think only about things down here on earth. For you died when Christ died, and your real life is hidden with Christ in God. And when Christ, who is your real life, is revealed to the whole world, you will share in all his glory.*

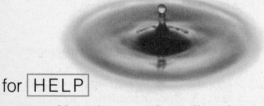

for HELP

Moses felt inadequate to be God's spokesman to the pharaoh of Egypt—he had no choice but to depend on God's help. This allowed God to show his strength through Moses' weakness. Exodus 4:12-15 explains:

> [The LORD said to Moses] "Now go, and do as I have told you. I will help you speak well, and I will tell you what to say." But Moses again pleaded, "Lord, please! Send someone else." Then the LORD became angry with Moses. "All right," he said. "What about your brother, Aaron the Levite? He is a good speaker. And look! He is on

his way to meet you now. And when he sees you, he will be very glad. You will talk to him, giving him the words to say. I will help both of you to speak clearly, and I will tell you what to do."

After three days of wandering in the desert without water, the Israelites complained to Moses. Exodus 15:25 reveals that Moses knew who to turn to for help.

So Moses cried out to the LORD for help, and the LORD showed him a branch. Moses took the branch and threw it into the water. This made the water good to drink.

David faced overwhelming obstacles and dangerous enemies many times in his life. He learned to ask God for help. In Psalm 145:18-19, David praised God for hearing his cries and helping him.

The LORD is close to all who call on him, yes, to all who call on him sincerely. He fulfills the desires of those who fear him; he hears their cries for help and rescues them.

In comic strips and cartoons, masked superheroes answer calls for help from those in distress. They rush quickly to the rescue at the first sign of trouble. We know, of course, that such characters exist only in fiction and in our imaginations. But at times, we want the cartoons to be true, especially when facing complex issues, giant problems, and difficult conflicts. We want someone to hear our frantic cries and run to our side.

These passages in Psalms declare that, in fact, someone *is* listening. Not an imaginary hero with superhuman powers, but a real person with *all* power and authority is standing near, ready to save. And more than simply rescuing individuals from temporal plights, this person, the Lord almighty, saves for all eternity.

God knows your situation and your desires. He stands close and ready to help.

FOR FURTHER STUDY
- God disciplines you to help you (Deuteronomy 8:5). *page 153*
- God hears those who ask him for help (Psalm 9:12). *page 435*
- Only God can help and protect you (Psalm 33:20). *page 446*
- Those who look to God for help will be filled with joy (Psalm 34:5). *page 447*
- God helps those who trust him (Psalm 37:5). *page 449*
- God can help you live in harmony with others (Romans 15:5). *page 877*
- Jesus can help you when you are tempted (Hebrews 2:18). *page 935*
- God gives help when you need it (Hebrews 4:16). *page 936*

for HOLINESS

The entire book of Leviticus emphasizes the holiness of God. Leviticus 19:2 clearly summarizes the message of the book:

Say this to the entire community of Israel: You must be holy because I, the LORD your God, am holy.

God calls his people to be holy, but he doesn't expect us to attain it on our own strength. In John

17:17, Jesus' prayer for his followers reveals that his Holy Spirit has the power to purify our minds and hearts.

"Make them pure and holy by teaching them your words of truth."

Paul reminded the early church in 1 Corinthians 1:2 that holiness only comes through the person and sacrifice of Jesus Christ.

We are writing to the church of God in Corinth, you who have been called by God to be his own holy people. He made you holy by means of Christ Jesus, just as he did all Christians everywhere—whoever calls upon the name of Jesus Christ, our Lord and theirs.

In a world saturated with evil, it is hard to imagine how a person can remain pure and holy.

The truth is, we can't. We cannot attain any level of righteousness on our own. Only God's power working through us can help us live according to God's law. Jesus, God's Son, is the only one who can remove our sins and give us power to resist temptation. As we invite God's Spirit into our hearts and lives, he cleans and purifies us. As we believe and obey God's Word, we become sanctified (set apart and made holy for God's glory).

Don't try to become holy on your own strength. Acknowledge your sinfulness. Ask God's Spirit to fill you and empower you. Then give God the praise for the good work he does in your life.

FOR FURTHER STUDY
- God alone is perfectly holy (Isaiah 6:3). *page 540*
- Believers need to work hard at avoiding sin (2 Corinthians 7:1). *page 896*

- Through Christ, God sees you as holy (Ephesians 5:25-27). *page 910*
- Christians should holy lives, just as God is holy (1 Peter 1:15). *page 949*

to know the HOLY SPIRIT

Romans 8:11 explains that the Holy Spirit serves as God's promise for those who put their faith in God. The Spirit lives in us now and, at the same time, is our guarantee of eternal life in the future.

The Spirit of God, who raised Jesus from the dead, lives in you. And just as he raised Christ from the dead, he will give life to your mortal body by this same Spirit living within you.

The Christians in Corinth were struggling to live out their faith in a hostile environment. Paul encouraged them in 1 Corinthians 2:10 saying:

But we know these things because God has revealed them to us by his Spirit, and his Spirit searches out everything and shows us even God's deep secrets.

In John 14:26, Jesus promised his followers that the Holy Spirit would remind them of the truth he had taught them. God's Spirit plays the same role today—he teaches and guards the truth.

"But when the Father sends the Counselor as my representative—and by the Counselor I mean the

Holy Spirit—he will teach you everything and will remind you of everything I myself have told you."

Jesus was teaching the disciples about the Holy Spirit, the "Spirit of truth." Translated as "Counselor" or "Comforter," the Greek word literally means "one who comes alongside." So this title pictures one person coming close to another, alongside, to guide (as on a path in the woods), to advise (as a lawyer in a court of law), to counsel (as a psychiatrist or simply a trusted friend), to speak words of concern (as in a hospital room), or to comfort (as at a graveside).

Clearly, God sends his Spirit to help all believers. The Spirit counsels and comforts by telling the truth about Jesus, and he assures believers of Christ's true identity, forgiveness of sins, love, and salvation.

Do you feel lost, wondering which way to turn? You are not alone. The Holy Spirit stands beside you and will guide you in God's way.

Do you feel accosted and accused? You're not alone. God's Spirit comes to your defense.

Do you feel confused, frustrated, anxious, or fearful? You're not alone. The Counselor is with you to give you hope and to tell you how to live.

Do you feel devastated by loss and overcome with grief? You're not alone. The Comforter is close, wrapping his arms around you and whispering words of love.

FOR FURTHER STUDY
- The Holy Spirit was involved in Creation (Genesis 1:2). *page 3*
- The Holy Spirit empowers leaders (Judges 3:10). *page 200*
- The Holy Spirit guides God's people (John 16:13). *page 829*

- The Holy Spirit empowers believers to be witnesses (Acts 1:8). *page 835*
- The Holy Spirit helps make our life a pleasing sacrifice to God (Romans 15:16). *page 877*
- The Holy Spirit give us new life (Titus 3:5). *page 932*

for HONESTY

When the prophet Nathan confronted David about his adultery with Bathsheba, David realized he could not hide his sin any longer. Psalm 51:3-6 is his honest confession of sin and his desire to know God's truth.

> *For I recognize my shameful deeds—they haunt me day and night. Against you, and you alone, have I sinned; I have done what is evil in your sight. You will be proved right in what you say, and your judgment against me is just. For I was born a sinner—yes, from the moment my mother conceived me. But you desire honesty from the heart, so you can teach me to be wise in my inmost being.*

David modeled honest prayer. In Psalm 143:7-8, he poured out his heart to God, expressing his fear, despair, and hopelessness.

> *Come quickly, LORD, and answer me, for my depression deepens. Don't turn away from me, or I will die. Let me hear of your unfailing love to me*

in the morning, for I am trusting you. Show me where to walk, for I have come to you in prayer.

The psalm writers expressed themselves honestly to God, sharing every feeling, from elation to despair. Here, while fighting fear and depression, David turned to God in desperation and poured out his soul.

Believers experience the whole range of emotions, the ups and the downs. The emotions are not wrong or sinful, they just are. But the response is critical. We can allow our emotions to pull us away from God or to push us toward him. In David's case, his depression moved him in God's direction. First he acknowledged his need and his total dependence on God, then he asked for God's guidance.

Don't try to hide your feelings from the Lord. Honestly express all of your fears and needs to him; then ask for his help. He will meet you where you are.

FOR FURTHER STUDY
• Honesty is commanded by God (Exodus 20:16). *page 63*
• Those who worship God should be characterized by honesty (Psalm 24:4). *page 442*
• God hates lies (Proverbs 6:16-17). *page 510*
• Be honest (Proverbs 19:1). *page 517*
• Christians should be known by their honesty (Matthew 5:37). *page 733*
• Lies flow out of an evil heart (Matthew 15:18-20). *page 743*
• Christians should put away dishonesty from their lives (Ephesians 4:25). *page 909*

for HOPE

When the psalm writer saw injustice all around him, he could have despaired and turned against God. Instead, he put his hope in God, trusting in God's holy character. Psalm 94:19 says:

> *When doubts filled my mind, your comfort gave me renewed hope and cheer.*

The apostle Paul deeply cared for the Christians in Rome. His prayer for his friends recorded in Romans 15:13 focuses on the hope they had through the power of God's Spirit.

> *So I pray that God, who gives you hope, will keep you happy and full of peace as you believe in him. May you overflow with hope through the power of the Holy Spirit.*

Finding himself surrounded by thousands of soldiers led by his own rebellious son, Absalom, David could have despaired. Instead of thinking that everyone was against him, however, he remembered that God was *for* him. Psalm 3:1-3 declares his hope in God:

> *O LORD, I have so many enemies; so many are against me. So many are saying, "God will never rescue him!" But you, O LORD, are a shield around me, my glory, and the one who lifts my head high.*

David wrote Psalm 3 while fleeing from Absalom. With his own son turning against him, David seemed to be surrounded by enemies. Those on his side expressed pessimism concerning the eventual outcome, doubting that even God could save him. Certainly David could have become utterly discouraged and without hope.

Yet he confidently wrote that God would protect him, destroy his enemies, and restore him to his rightful place on the throne. David had no idea how this would happen—he was devastated politically, physically, and emotionally. But he knew who was in charge of his life and destiny. David's hope rested not on his abilities or the strength of his armies but on his sovereign God.

Many seem to spend their lives running and hiding, upset about the past, anxious about the present, and worried about the future. Seeing enemies everywhere, even in themselves, they hang their heads in shame and despair. David could have given up; instead, he found courage and hope in God.

God is your shield, too. Trust him. Put your full hope in him, and he will meet your every need.

FOR FURTHER STUDY
- God gives hope to the needy (Psalm 9:18). *page 435*
- We need to place our hope in God (Psalm 25:5). *page 442*
- Hope in God enables us to wait quietly before him (Psalm 62:5). *page 461*
- Put your hope in God's Word (Psalm 119:43, 147). *pages 493, 495*
- Christians always have hope that God is working in everything (Romans 8:28). *page 871*
- Jesus' resurrection gives hope (1 Corinthians 6:14). *page 882*

- Our hope in Christ is not merely for our earthly life but for eternity (1 Corinthians 15:19). *page 890*
- Believers have the hope of eternal life (Titus 1:1-2). *page 931*

for HUMILITY

The Israelites had a chronic problem of pride. They continually failed to admit their need for God and chose to trust in their own strength instead. Time and time again, God had to show them the foolishness of their ways. He had to humble them for their own good. In Deuteronomy 8:16-18, Moses reminded the Israelites of the importance of humility.

> *He fed you with manna in the wilderness, a food unknown to your ancestors. He did this to humble you and test you for your own good. He did it so you would never think that it was your own strength and energy that made you wealthy. Always remember that it is the LORD your God who gives you power to become rich, and he does it to fulfill the covenant he made with your ancestors.*

Proverbs 11:2 offers a simple truth we can hold onto—if we humble ourselves before God, we will gain wisdom.

> *Pride leads to disgrace, but with humility comes wisdom.*

God works best through humble people. When we admit that we are helpless and hopeless without him, God can use us to do great things for his Kingdom. James 4:10 says:

> *When you bow down before the Lord and admit your dependence on him, he will lift you up and give you honor.*

FOR FURTHER STUDY
- God hears the prayers of the humble (2 Chronicles 7:14). *page 357*
- God saves those who are humble (Psalm 18:27). *page 439*
- God supports humble people (Psalm 147:6). *page 505*
- God will bless the humble (Isaiah 66:2). *page 577*
- God will exalt the humble (Luke 18:14). *page 803*
- Be humble in dealing with others (Philippians 2:1-11). *page 913*

to avoid HYPOCRISY

Jesus warned his followers in Luke 12:1-2 to avoid the sin of hypocrisy. Although we may be able to hide our true motives and intentions now, God sees through us and will reveal the truth in time. When we are tempted to pretend to be something we are not, we should remember that God sees the heart—his opinion is the one that matters most.

> *Jesus turned first to his disciples and warned them, "Beware of the yeast of the Pharisees— beware of their hypocrisy. The time is coming*

when everything will be revealed; all that is secret will be made public."

Peter wrote a letter of encouragement and admonition to Jewish Christians who were suffering for their faith. His words in 1 Peter 2:1 remind us of the importance of avoiding hypocrisy. God's people should be characterized by truthfulness and humility.

So get rid of all malicious behavior and deceit. Don't just pretend to be good! Be done with hypocrisy and jealousy and backstabbing.

FOR FURTHER STUDY
- Do not associate with hypocrites (Psalm 26:4). *page 443*
- God hates hypocrisy in worship (Isaiah 29:13). *page 554*
- Hypocrites pretend to be devoted to God (Ezekiel 33:31-32). *pages 654-655*
- God finds hypocrites repulsive (Matthew 23:27-28). *page 752*
- God will punish hypocrisy (Luke 20:46-47). *page 806*
- Hypocrites are worthless for doing anything good (Titus 1:16). *page 931*

to avoid IMMORALITY

Our bodies are not our own—we belong to God. Our bodies are the dwelling place of God's Spirit. First Corinthians 6:19-20 explains that it is the Spirit living in us who can give us power and strength to avoid sinning against God with our bodies.

> *Or don't you know that your body is the temple of the Holy Spirit, who lives in you and was given to you by God? You do not belong to yourself, for God bought you with a high price. So you must honor God with your body.*

Sexual immorality brings pain and destruction to God's people and his church. We should do all we can to help one another avoid this sin that should have no place in our lives. Paul warns the church in Ephesians 5:3 to avoid even the hint of immorality or impropriety.

> *Let there be no sexual immorality, impurity, or greed among you. Such sins have no place among God's people.*

FOR FURTHER STUDY
- Compromises can lead to immorality (Judges 3:1-11). *page 200*
- Immorality flows out of an evil heart (Matthew 15:19). *page 743*
- Stay away from immoral Christians (1 Corinthians 5:9-11). *page 882*
- Immorality should have no place among Christians (Ephesians 4:17-19). *page 909*

for INTEGRITY

David knew he had sinned and that he could not remain faithful on his own strength. But he believed in God's forgiveness. Second Samuel 22:25-27 is David's song of praise to God for helping him live with integrity, even in the most trying times.

The LORD rewarded me for doing right, because of my innocence in his sight. To the faithful you show yourself faithful; to those with integrity you show integrity. To the pure you show yourself pure, but to the wicked you show yourself hostile.

Following King David's example, the people of Israel gave generously to the temple building project. In 1 Chronicles 29:17, David acknowledged that God was pleased when his people lived with integrity.

I know, my God, that you examine our hearts and rejoice when you find integrity there. You know I have done all this with good motives, and I have watched your people offer their gifts willingly and joyously.

Jehoshaphat, king of Judah, appointed judges, priests, and Levites to serve as leaders to rule over the people and to administer the law. He instructed them in 2 Chronicles 19:9 to live carefully, honestly, and with integrity.

"You must always act in the fear of the LORD, with integrity and with undivided hearts."

Appearances can be deceiving. People can put on a good face whenever they think others are watching, but then let down their guard in private. They may fool a lot of people and win the undeserved respect of their peers, but God sees past their façade.

God wants his people to live differently. The Bible tells us to live with integrity, even when people are not watching us. Integrity—being what we say we are—is the opposite of hypocrisy. Integrity keeps us from claiming to be upright when our hearts are far from God.

Do you make the right choices, even when no one is looking? Remember, God can see deep into your heart. He sees your motives and attitudes.

Choose to live with integrity. Even if no one notices you making the right choices, God notices, and he will be pleased. And in the end, his opinion is the one that matters.

FOR FURTHER STUDY

- Integrity takes effort and discipline (Psalm 101:3-8). *page 482*
- Integrity provides a solid foundation for life (Proverbs 10:9). *page 511*
- Leaders prove their integrity at home (1 Timothy 3:4-5). *page 925*
- Leaders in the church must have integrity (Titus 1:7). *page 931*
- We must maintain integrity in teaching others (Titus 2:7). *page 931*

for INTIMACY WITH GOD

In an effort to fill our longing for God, we often drink deeply at the wrong wells and fountains, coming away with a thirst even deeper than before. Long ago the prophet Jeremiah brought this word from the Lord, as recorded in Jeremiah 2:13:

For my people have done two evil things: They have forsaken me—the fountain of living water. And they have dug for themselves cracked cisterns that can hold no water at all!

Jesus told a woman at the well in Samaria that he offered living water—spiritual water that could quench people's thirst for God forever. John 4:13-14 records Jesus' explanation to the woman:

"People soon become thirsty again after drinking this water. But the water I give them takes away thirst altogether. It becomes a perpetual spring within them, giving them eternal life."

Our God is a personal, knowable God who desires a close relationship with the people he created. James 4:8 tells us that we can develop intimacy with him by drawing close and listening to his voice.

Draw close to God, and God will draw close to you.

First John 3:1 tells us that God loves us and calls us his children—what a profound promise! This is not just a future reality, it is true *now*.

See how very much our heavenly Father loves us, for he allows us to be called his children, and we really are! But the people who belong to this world don't know God, so they don't understand that we are his children.

Each person is created with a God-shaped vacuum, an emptiness that only he can fill—a deep thirst for God.

We thirst for so many things—for significance, success, comfort, peace, wisdom. But our real thirst is for a closeness to our Creator who alone can give wholeness and peace. Only God can satisfy our deepest longings.

God offers us water that can satisfy our deepest thirsts and longings. All we need to do is come and drink.

FOR FURTHER STUDY
- Spending time with God leads to intimacy with him (Psalm 1:2). *page 432*
- God draws near to those who seek him (Psalm 75:1). *pages 468-469*
- Virtue is essential for lasting intimacy (Proverbs 31:10-12). *pages 524-525*
- God wants an intimate relationship with you (Hosea 2:16-20). *page 685*
- God will always be present with his people (Matthew 28:20). *page 759*

for INTIMACY WITH OTHERS

Solomon had everything his heart desired—wisdom and wealth beyond compare. But he knew each of us needs other people because God created us for intimacy and companionship. Ecclesiastes 4:9, 11-12 says:

> Two people can accomplish more than twice as much as one; they get a better return for their labor. And on a cold night, two under the same blanket can gain warmth from each other. But how can one be warm alone? A person standing alone can be attacked and defeated, but two can stand back-to-back and conquer. Three are even better, for a triple-braided cord is not easily broken.

Hebrews 10:25 reveals that some of the early Christians had begun to neglect their relationships with one another. The writer highlights the importance of working hard to maintain intimacy with other believers for mutual support and accountability.

> And let us not neglect our meeting together, as some people do, but encourage and warn each other, especially now that the day of his coming back again is drawing near.

Sometimes people isolate themselves. When dealing with a difficult problem or struggling through a life-wrenching tragedy, they pull back from others and just stay away. It seems too painful to talk about, so they want to be left alone. Or perhaps they have sinned deeply and fear embarrassment or condemnation. Yet during those times of difficulty and conflict they need others the most, especially friends who will listen, comfort, affirm, and point them to Christ.

That is exactly what the church should be—a place where believers can find intimacy, a place where believers encourage and strengthen each other, a place where people find acceptance, love, and God's grace.

Evidently, according to the passage in Hebrews, some had gotten out of their churchgoing habit. They needed the body of Christ, however, considering the time in which they lived and their proximity to "the day of his coming back again"— Christ's return and the final judgment.

Today, we stand even closer to that day, and certainly we live in difficult times. More than ever we need to develop intimacy with others. We need others who know us and who know the Lord; we need to meet together regularly for worship, instruction, fellowship, challenge, and strengthening.

What keeps you from your Christian brothers and sisters? Don't stay away any longer. Do what you can to develop close relationships with those people who can help you in your Christian walk.

FOR FURTHER STUDY
• Intimacy can be ruined by jealousy (Genesis 26:12-16).
  page 21

to overcome JEALOUSY

If life hasn't treated us fairly, we may think that we have a right to be jealous of others, especially those who have more than they deserve. But Proverbs 14:30 warns that jealousy will only harm us, robbing us of inner peace.

A relaxed attitude lengthens life; jealousy rots it away.

Proverbs 27:4 describes jealousy as a powerful enemy. We shouldn't allow envy to take root in our hearts; it will destroy us.

Anger is cruel, and wrath is like a flood, but who can survive the destructiveness of jealousy?

Jealousy is the tool of the Devil. Seeking God's wisdom can save us from it. James 3:15-16 admonishes believers to guard against the sin of jealousy.

For jealousy and selfishness are not God's kind of wisdom. Such things are earthly, unspiritual, and motivated by the Devil. For wherever there is jealousy and selfish ambition, there you will find disorder and every kind of evil.

FOR FURTHER STUDY
- Jealousy can destroy a person (Job 5:2). *page 414*
- Being jealous is foolish (Ecclesiastes 4:4). *page 527*
- Jealousy can cause you to act rashly (Acts 7:9). *page 841*
- Jealousy characterizes sinful people (Romans 1:29). *page 866*
- Do not envy other Christians (Galatians 5:26). *page 906*
- Jealousy has no place in a Christian's life (Titus 3:3). *page 932*

to know JESUS CHRIST

Before God sent his Son to earth, people's ability to know God was limited. But when God took on human form, in the person of Jesus Christ, people could know him fully and tangibly. John 1:14 describes Jesus as completely human, someone we can know personally and intimately.

So the Word became human and lived here on earth among us. He was full of unfailing love and faithfulness. And we have seen his glory, the glory of the only Son of the Father.

In this powerful picture in Revelation 3:20, Jesus stands at the door of the church, knocking. He wants to enter, to be welcomed to fellowship with believers, to know them and be known by them.

> *"Look! Here I stand at the door and knock. If you hear me calling and open the door, I will come in, and we will share a meal as friends."*

Revelation chapter 3 shows that our Lord Jesus desires to enter our hearts and lives. Notice, however, that he allows us to open the door for ourselves. Jesus doesn't force his will on us, pounding at the door or prying it open; instead, he stands and knocks politely.

The church at Laodicea had become "luke-warm"; that is, they had allowed their passion for Christ to cool and had become enamored with themselves and their wealth instead. Eventually, Jesus was no longer with them. Thus, he was standing on the outside, knocking, hoping to get their attention so that he might enter and change their lives.

Where is Jesus for you? Outside or inside? Is he a stranger, or do you "share meals" together? Do you seek daily to know him and his will for you? What concerns occupy your thoughts? Relationships? Career? Possessions and power? Perhaps even survival? Do they threaten to push Jesus to the fringe of your life?

Whatever your situation, know that the Lord is standing near. Through the din and demands, hear his gentle knock. Push through the clutter and open the door. Then welcome Christ and give him his rightful place in your life.

FOR FURTHER STUDY
- Jesus is the Son of God (Luke 1:35). *pages 780-781*
- Jesus is God (John 1:1-5). *page 812*

- Jesus gives life (John 10:10). *page 823*
- Jesus is the Good Shepherd (John 10:11). *page 823*
- Jesus is the only way to God (John 14:6). *page 827*
- Jesus is the author of life (Acts 3:15). *page 837*
- Jesus is the wisdom of God (1 Corinthians 1:21-24). *page 879*
- Jesus is faithful (2 Timothy 2:13). *page 929*
- Jesus is holy (Hebrews 7:26). *page 938*
- Jesus is the Lamb of God (Revelation 21:22). *page 977*

for JOY

King David and the leaders and officers of Israel gave willingly and generously to the work of building God's temple. First Chronicles 29:9 describes the joy God gives his people when they obey and honor him.

> *The people rejoiced over the offerings, for they had given freely and wholeheartedly to the LORD, and King David was filled with joy.*

The psalm writer knew the difference between true joy that comes from knowing and trusting God and temporal happiness that comes when life is easy. Psalm 4:7 declares that the joy God gives is the best:

> *You have given me greater joy than those who have abundant harvests of grain and wine.*

In Isaiah 49, the prophet brought bad and good news to God's people. The bad news was that they would be taken captive by a foreign power, but the good news was that eventually the nation would be restored. The best news was that whether captive or free, God would be with them, giving them comfort, hope, and joy. Verse 13 says:

Sing for joy, O heavens! Rejoice, O earth! Burst into song, O mountains! For the LORD has comforted his people and will have compassion on them in their sorrow.

Just as God promised to give hope and joy to the people of Israel, both in good times and bad times, he promises to give us *all* we need, at *all* times.

Do you feel hemmed in, trapped, a captive to your unrelenting schedule, and assaulted by a host of enemies who threaten to steal your joy? Or do you feel desperate as you struggle with physical pain, financial demands, or interpersonal conflicts? Listen to God's Word. Isaiah says that the Lord comforts his people and will give them joy.

God hasn't forgotten you; in fact, he sees you right now and knows what you are going through.

Make your next move toward him, and he will give you joy!

FOR FURTHER STUDY

- God's presence should bring you joy (Psalm 16:8-9). *page 437*
- Joy comes from fearing the Lord (Psalm 112:1). *page 490*
- Obeying God will lead to joy (Psalm 119:2). *page 492*
- Jesus promises joy especially for those who are faithful in difficulty (Matthew 5:3-10). *page 732*
- The Holy Spirit produces joy in believers (Galatians 5:22). *page 906*

- Joy should not depend on circumstances (Philippians 4:12). *page 914*
- Sometimes joy comes through pain (Hebrews 12:2). *page 942*
- Hard times can be an opportunity for joy (James 1:2). *page 944*

for JUSTICE

Psalm 11:7 describes God as righteous and just. In the midst of unfairness, we can trust these aspects of God's character.

> *For the LORD is righteous, and he loves justice.*
> *Those who do what is right will see his face.*

In an attempt to comfort Job in his time of suffering and pain, his friend, Elihu, proclaimed a truth that we can depend on even today. Job 34:12 declares:

> *There is no truer statement than this: God will not do wrong. The Almighty cannot twist justice.*

Isaiah received a prophetic message from the Lord to give to the nation of Israel. God's words to the Israelites in Isaiah 1:17 remind us of the importance of seeking justice.

> *Learn to do good. Seek justice. Help the oppressed.*
> *Defend the orphan. Fight for the rights of widows.*

God is concerned about justice in our world—this theme runs through the entire Bible. It is also clear that he expects his people to encourage, defend, and plead for the needy in society. Thus, obvious personal applications flow from Scripture as we consider the oppressed, fatherless, and widows with whom we come into contact. "What can we do to seek justice for them?" we should ask.

Beneath God's words of admonition in this verse, however, lies another very personal truth, for this passage reveals a marvelous fact about God's nature. Because God wants justice, he will be on our side when *we* are oppressed and when *we* lose father, mother, or spouse. He will be fighting *for us* and will be *with us* through it all, encouraging us, defending us, and pleading our case.

So when you feel abused, abandoned, and alone, as though no one cares, remember that you worship a God of justice—supreme, almighty, the righteous judge—and he is on your side. And, oh yes, don't forget to encourage others with that truth as well.

FOR FURTHER STUDY
- Justice should not be twisted to please others (Exodus 23:2). *page 65*
- God blesses those who uphold justice (Deuteronomy 16:19-20). *page 160*
- You must never hold back justice (Deuteronomy 27:19). *page 167*
- God will judge the world justly (Psalm 9:8). *page 435*
- Jesus' death satisfied justice for your sins (Romans 3:25-26). *page 867*

for KINDNESS

Ephesians 4:32 encourages us to extend the same kindness to others that we receive from God.

Instead, be kind to each other, tenderhearted, forgiving one another, just as God through Christ has forgiven you.

Kindness comes more easily to some than others, but most of us struggle with showing kindness to difficult people. Second Timothy 2:24 highlights the importance of showing kindness to *all* people, even those who do not return the favor.

The Lord's servants must not quarrel but must be kind to everyone. They must be able to teach effectively and be patient with difficult people.

FOR FURTHER STUDY
- Be kind to people who treat you wrongly (1 Thessalonians 5:15). *page 921*
- God shows great kindness (1 Peter 5:10). *page 952*
- Being kind takes effort (2 Peter 1:5-7). *page 953*

for KNOWLEDGE

Knowledge does not come easily. Proverbs 2:3-6 says to seek wisdom earnestly and persistently. God will reward our efforts—he will give us knowledge if we demonstrate our desire for it.

> Cry out for insight and understanding. Search for them as you would for lost money or hidden treasure. Then you will understand what it means to fear the LORD, and you will gain knowledge of God. For the LORD grants wisdom! From his mouth come knowledge and understanding.

Jesus, in Matthew 13:12, warns that knowledge is not enough, God desires obedience. Only when we apply the knowledge God has given us will he reveal more.

> "To those who are open to my teaching, more understanding will be given, and they will have an abundance of knowledge. But to those who are not listening, even what they have will be taken away from them."

FOR FURTHER STUDY
- A prerequisite to knowledge is a proper regard for God (Proverbs 1:7-9). page 507
- There is a difference between knowing God and knowing about God (Matthew 15:9). page 743

- Knowledge of Jesus is not enough for salvation (Mark 3:11). *page 762*
- Knowledge of the Bible is not enough for salvation (John 3:10-11). *page 814*

for LEADERSHIP

When Jehoshaphat appointed leaders for the people of Israel, he told them they would represent God in their decisions. His words of encouragement and warning in 2 Chronicles 19:5-7 reveal that leadership is a solemn responsibility.

> *He appointed judges throughout the nation in all the fortified cities, and he gave them these instructions: "Always think carefully before pronouncing judgment. Remember that you do not judge to please people but to please the LORD. He will be with you when you render the verdict in each case that comes before you. Fear the LORD and judge with care, for the LORD our God does not tolerate perverted justice, partiality, or the taking of bribes."*

Second Timothy 2 describes the kind of person fit for leadership. Those who want to become leaders should ask God to develop these traits in them: honesty, kindness, patience, purity, and integrity. Verses 24-25 explain:

> *The Lord's servants must not quarrel but must be kind to everyone. They must be able to teach effec-*

tively and be patient with difficult people. They should gently teach those who oppose the truth.

Leaders who teach God's Word have an even greater responsibility to use their authority carefully. Paul urged his friend Titus to model Christian character and to guard his integrity. People watch Christian leaders very carefully—they must be above reproach. Titus 2:7-8 and 15 state:

> *And you yourself must be an example to them by doing good deeds of every kind. Let everything you do reflect the integrity and seriousness of your teaching. Let your teaching be so correct that it can't be criticized. Then those who want to argue will be ashamed because they won't have anything bad to say about us. You must teach these things and encourage your people to do them, correcting them when necessary. You have the authority to do this, so don't let anyone ignore you or disregard what you say.*

FOR FURTHER STUDY
- Leaders should be trustworthy (Exodus 18:21). *page 61*
- People need good leadership (Numbers 27:16-17). *page 137*
- Leaders should receive advice (Proverbs 11:14). *page 512*
- Leaders must serve others (Matthew 20:26-28). *page 748*
- Leaders should sacrifice for others (John 10:11). *page 823*
- Leaders should be obeyed (Romans 13:1-5). *pages 875-876*

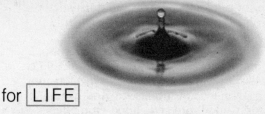

for LIFE

Life is miraculous and mysterious. Genesis 2:7 reveals that our bodies are "dust" until God chooses to breath life into us. He alone is the giver of life!

> *And the LORD God formed a man's body from the dust of the ground and breathed into it the breath of life. And the man became a living person.*

God gives physical life as well as spiritual life. Isaiah 55:1-2 describes the nourishment God provides for the soul.

> *"Is anyone thirsty? Come and drink—even if you have no money! Come, take your choice of wine or milk—it's all free! Why spend your money on food that does not give you strength? Why pay for food that does you no good? Listen, and I will tell you where to get food that is good for the soul!"*

When Nicodemus came to Jesus searching for spiritual truth, Jesus explained to him that he needed to be "born again." John 3:3 teaches us that real life comes through repentance and spiritual rebirth.

> *Jesus replied, "I assure you, unless you are born again, you can never see the Kingdom of God."*

Imagine a bright oasis with tall palms, clear springs, and abundant food and drink. Offering satisfaction and even life, this cherished spot in the sands would draw hungry and thirsty desert wanderers. Desperate and needy, they would expend every ounce of strength to get there.

Just as dry throats and parched lips yearn for drink, and empty stomachs and starved bodies cry for food, spiritually starved and thirsty men and women strain toward sustenance. And like a glorious oasis, God's Word gives hope. God offers satisfaction, renewal, real soul food—life. Other offers entice, but they prove to be mirages. This oasis is real.

Do you thirst? Drink God's Water of Life. Are you hungry? Pull up to his banquet table, and feast on his goodness. There you will find real life.

FOR FURTHER STUDY
- God carefully creates each person (Psalm 139:13-14). *pages 501-502*
- Life should be enjoyed (Ecclesiastes 11:9). *page 531*
- God plans the lives of people before they are born (Jeremiah 1:5). *page 579*
- Jesus came to give abundant life (John 10:10). *page 823*
- Believers should live worthy of their Christian calling (Ephesians 4:1). *page 909*
- Christ is the reason for living (Philippians 1:21). *page 913*
- Your life should honor God (Colossians 3:17). *page 918*

for LIGHT

Fears can overwhelm and enslave, but God's light is brighter than the darkness of fear. His light brings liberation and freedom. Psalm 27:1 declares that God's light dispels all fear.

> *The LORD is my light and my salvation— so why should I be afraid? The LORD protects me from danger— so why should I tremble?*

We can be vessels of God's light to the world. Second Corinthians 4:6-7 encourages us to allow God's brilliant light to shine in and through us, so that others can experience God's glory.

> *For God, who said, "Let there be light in the darkness," has made us understand that this light is the brightness of the glory of God that is seen in the face of Jesus Christ. But this precious treasure—this light and power that now shine within us—is held in perishable containers, that is, in our weak bodies. So everyone can see that our glorious power is from God and is not our own.*

FOR FURTHER STUDY

- Light comes from God (Genesis 1:3). *page 3*
- God's Word enlightens your path (Psalm 13:3). *page 436*
- God can turn darkness into light (Isaiah 42:16). *page 563*
- Christians are the light of the world (Matthew 5:14). *page 732*
- Jesus is the light of the world (John 9:5). *pages 821-822*

- Christians are children of light (1 Thessalonians 5:5). *page 921*

to LISTEN TO GOD

In his farewell speech to the Israelites, Samuel highlighted the importance of listening to God's voice. We learn from his words in 1 Samuel 12:14 that listening to God is the secret to experiencing his presence and blessing in our lives.

"Now if you will fear and worship the LORD and listen to his voice, and if you do not rebel against the LORD's commands, and if you and your king follow the LORD your God, then all will be well."

Many people harden their hearts to God's voice. They assume wrongly that if they listen, God will ask them to do something too difficult. Listening to God involves trusting in his good character and his ability to do what is best for us. We should obey God's word in Hebrews 3:7 and open our hearts to God's voice.

That is why the Holy Spirit says, "Today you must listen to his voice."

FOR FURTHER STUDY
- Listening is an important aspect of spiritual growth (Deuteronomy 5:1). *page 151*
- God speaks if you will listen (1 Kings 19:11-13). *page 291*
- Listening to God results in wisdom (Proverbs 1:23). *page 507*

- Listening must be followed by obedience (Luke 6:49). *page 788*
- Listening is an important part of communication (James 1:19). *page 945*

for help in times of
LONELINESS

God created us as relational beings—he wants us to turn to other people for friendship, support, and help. This truth is revealed early in Scripture, in Genesis 2:18, when God created a companion for Adam.

> *And the LORD God said, "It is not good for the man to be alone. I will make a companion who will help him."*

In Psalm 68:6, David praised God for the way he cares for lonely people.

> *God places the lonely in families; he sets the prisoners free and gives them joy. But for rebels, there is only famine and distress.*

Ecclesiastes 4:9-10 gives advice to the lonely—reach out to others for help. Look for friends who can comfort you and help you through your loneliness.

> *Two people can accomplish more than twice as much as one; they get a better return for their labor. If one person falls, the other can reach out and help. But people who are alone when they fall are in real trouble.*

Even the best of friends sometimes fail us in our time of need—but God never fails. Peter reminds us in 1 Peter 5:12 that God will be with us and will help us "no matter what happens."

I have written this short letter to you with the help of Silas, whom I consider a faithful brother. My purpose in writing is to encourage you and assure you that the grace of God is with you no matter what happens.

Do you ever feel forgotten—alone in a crowd, in the increasing pace of life, or even in the culture of the corporation? Feeling lonely and anonymous, you may wonder whether anybody knows or cares.

God does. He remembers your name and his promise to be with you, to guide you, and to bring you home. Now it's up to you to remember your Lord and his love for you and then to rest secure and hope in him.

FOR FURTHER STUDY
- God encourages the lonely (1 Kings 19:14-18). *page 291*
- God does not crush the lonely (Isaiah 42:1-7). *page 563*
- Jesus is always with you (Matthew 28:20). *page 759*

for help in dealing with LOSS

God does not promise that we will never experience loss, but he does promise to comfort us by
giving us strength, encouragement, and hope to
cope with our loss. Second Thessalonians 2:16-17
is a wonderful prayer that offers comfort to those
who trust in Jesus.

> *May our Lord Jesus Christ and God our Father,*
> *who loved us and in his special favor gave us*
> *everlasting comfort and good hope, comfort your*
> *hearts and give you strength in every good thing*
> *you do and say.*

The comfort God gives us is so full and deep that
we can extend it to others. Second Corinthians
1:4-5, 7 describes the way God wants us to help
others who experience loss.

> *He comforts us in all our troubles so that we can*
> *comfort others. When others are troubled, we will*
> *be able to give them the same comfort God has*
> *given us. You can be sure that the more we suffer*
> *for Christ, the more God will shower us with his*
> *comfort through Christ. We are confident that as*
> *you share in suffering, you will also share God's*
> *comfort.*

After many words of somber warning to the
people of Israel, Jeremiah offered a glimpse of
hope. Jeremiah 31:13 describes God's eagerness to

bless his people, to comfort them in times of loss, and to turn their sadness to joy.

The young women will dance for joy, and the men—old and young—will join in the celebration. I will turn their mourning into joy. I will comfort them and exchange their sorrow for rejoicing.

Have you ever danced at a funeral? That would be unthinkable, absurd. Funerals are times of somber reflection, sorrow, mourning. We expect funerals to bring sadness and tears, not joy and celebration.

We mourn for many reasons, and each painful loss tears our emotions and causes us to regret past actions and missed opportunities and to wonder what might have been. Certainly nothing hurts more than the death of a loved one—we miss our fiancée or spouse or child or friend, and we long to hear that familiar voice and to feel the person's touch.

Through Jeremiah, however, we learn that God will turn "mourning into joy." That's God's plan. Because we know him, our ultimate destiny is heaven, and we have the solid assurance that one day all sickness, death, and sorrow will be banished—we will be perfect and complete. Actually, all of this earth, including our pain, is temporary, but our joy will last forever.

Whatever your loss, keep your eyes on Christ and gain God's eternal perspective.

FOR FURTHER STUDY
- God hears your cries and comforts you (Psalm 10:17). *page 436*
- God is close to you in your pain (Psalm 23:4). *page 442*
- God's Word comforts you (Psalm 119:52). *page 493*

for LOVE

The Israelites had just escaped from slavery in Egypt when God gave them the Ten Commandments. He promised to "lavish" his love on them, if they would obey these laws. Exodus 20:6 is an astounding promise of God's love and faithfulness to his people.

> *But I lavish my love on those who love me and obey my commands, even for a thousand generations.*

It is all too easy for us to feel separated from God, all alone, and unloved, but Romans 8:35-39 assures us that it is *impossible* to escape God's love, even if we don't *feel* his love.

> *Can anything ever separate us from Christ's love? Does it mean he no longer loves us if we have trouble or calamity, or are persecuted, or are hungry or cold or in danger or threatened with death? (Even the Scriptures say, "For your sake we are killed every day; we are being slaughtered like sheep.") No, despite all these things, overwhelming victory is ours through Christ, who loved us. And I am convinced that nothing can ever separate us from his love. Death can't, and life can't.*

131

The angels can't, and the demons can't. Our fears for today, our worries about tomorrow, and even the powers of hell can't keep God's love away. Whether we are high above the sky or in the deepest ocean, nothing in all creation will ever be able to separate us from the love of God that is revealed in Christ Jesus our Lord.

Despite our sinfulness, God pours out his love on us! The psalm writer treasured this truth—he praised God for his awesome, unfailing love in Psalm 36:7-9.

How precious is your unfailing love, O God! All humanity finds shelter in the shadow of your wings. You feed them from the abundance of your own house, letting them drink from your rivers of delight. For you are the fountain of life, the light by which we see.

In times of pain and in times of joy, God envelops us in his love. In Psalm 36, David uses a variety of images to describe the reality of God's love:

Shelter in the shadow of your wings—like a baby bird who finds safety in the nest, we are protected by God.

Feed them from the abundance of your own house—God invites us as welcomed guests to his lavish banquet table overflowing with blessings.

Drink from your rivers of delight—God's endless river brings refreshing, thirst-quenching joy.

You are the fountain of life—God is the only source of eternal life, and we can know him!

The light by which we see—God brings us out of darkness and reveals truth.

The picture is clear. God's love never fails, and you can experience it now. Rest secure in the knowledge that nothing can separate you from God's love.

FOR FURTHER STUDY
- God's love never fails (Exodus 15:13). *page 58*
- God constantly loves those who obey him (Deuteronomy 7:9). *page 152*
- God's love pursues you (Psalm 23:6). *page 442*
- Jesus showed genuine love for people (Mark 10:21). *page 770*
- God's love is beyond human understanding (Ephesians 3:18). *page 909*
- God is love (1 John 4:16). *page 958*

for LOYALTY

Second Chronicles 15:14-15 presents a beautiful picture of God's people declaring their renewed sense of loyalty to him. Allegiance to God must come first; he alone deserves our wholehearted commitment. Nothing should interfere with our loyalty to God.

> *They shouted out their oath of loyalty to the LORD with trumpets blaring and horns sounding. All were happy about this covenant, for they had entered into it with all their hearts. Eagerly they sought after God, and they found him. And the LORD gave them rest from their enemies on every side.*

Proverbs 17:17 reveals that loyalty is a test of true friendship. To be a loyal friend, we should stick around, even when things get rough.

> *A friend is always loyal, and a brother is born to help in time of need.*

A loyal friend is a treasure! When you demonstrate loyalty, people will want to have you for a friend. Proverbs 19:22 describes the appeal of loyalty.

> *Loyalty makes a person attractive. And it is better to be poor than dishonest.*

FOR FURTHER STUDY
- Loyalty is important (Proverbs 3:3). *page 508*
- You cannot divide your loyalty (Matthew 6:24). *page 734*
- Jesus wants your loyalty (Luke 12:51-53). *page 798*
- God's people should be loyal to him (Ephesians 1:1). *page 907*
- There must be loyalty in marriage (Hebrews 13:4). *page 943*

for a good MARRIAGE

Some of the Corinthian Christians wanted to divorce their non-believing spouses, but Paul affirmed the commitment of marriage in 1 Corinthians 7:14. God wants us to make marriage work—it is a lifelong commitment.

> *For the Christian wife brings holiness to her marriage, and the Christian husband brings holi-*

ness to his marriage. Otherwise, your children would not have a godly influence, but now they are set apart for him.

Hebrews 13:4 also emphasizes the sanctity of the marriage relationship. If we build our marriage on God's Word and remain faithful, we honor God.

Give honor to marriage, and remain faithful to one another in marriage. God will surely judge people who are immoral and those who commit adultery.

FOR FURTHER STUDY
- God hates divorce (Malachi 2:16). *page 725*
- Two people become one through marriage (Mark 10:2-12). *page 770*
- Angels do not get married (Mark 12:25). *page 773*
- Married partners should meet the needs of their own spouse (1 Corinthians 7:2-5). *page 883*
- Married partners are united to each other for life (1 Corinthians 7:39). *page 884*
- A Christian wife can witness to her non-Christian husband through obedience (1 Peter 3:1-6). *page 951*

for MEANING IN LIFE

The book of Ecclesiastes describes Solomon's search for the meaning of life. His words in Ecclesiastes 2:26 affirm that true happiness is found in seeking God and his wisdom.

God gives wisdom, knowledge, and joy to those who please him. But if a sinner becomes wealthy,

*God takes the wealth away and gives it to those
who please him. Even this, however, is meaningless, like chasing the wind.*

Solomon recognized the human need for meaning
and fulfillment. Ecclesiastes 6:3 speaks of the futil-
ity of living without discovering the meaning of
life.

*A man might have a hundred children and live
to be very old. But if he finds no satisfaction in
life and in the end does not even get a decent
burial, I say he would have been better off born
dead.*

Ecclesiastes 12:13-14 states Solomon's triumphant
conclusion: The meaning of life is found in obeying God.

*Here is my final conclusion: Fear God and obey
his commands, for this is the duty of every
person. God will judge us for everything we do,
including every secret thing, whether good or
bad.*

FOR FURTHER STUDY
- God's presence brings true joy and fulfillment (Psalm
  16:11). *page 437*
- Those who seek God will discover the meaning of life
  (Psalm 22:26). *page 441*
- Obeying God brings fulfillment (1 Corinthians 9:18). *page
  885*
- Doing your best brings a sense of satisfaction (Galatians
  6:4). *page 906*

for MERCY

Jeremiah 31:3 is a statement of love and restoration that comes after dark prophetic predictions of God punishing his people. Even when God allows us to suffer the consequences of our sin, he does not withhold his mercy.

> *Long ago the LORD said to Israel: "I have loved you, my people, with an everlasting love. With unfailing love I have drawn you to myself."*

Everyone deserves to be punished for sin, but God's punishment is always tempered with mercy because of his great love for us. Ephesians 2:4-5 explains that we are saved from our sin *only* because of God's mercy.

> *But God is so rich in mercy, and he loved us so very much, that even while we were dead because of our sins, he gave us life when he raised Christ from the dead. (It is only by God's special favor that you have been saved!)*

Although we do not deserve to enter his presence, God wants us to come boldly before him. Hebrews 4:16 promises that we will find mercy and grace— *all* that we need, exactly *when* we need it.

> *So let us come boldly to the throne of our gracious God. There we will receive his mercy, and we will find grace to help us when we need it.*

God loves to show mercy! He eagerly waits for us to repent so that he can shower us with forgiveness. Micah 7:18 declares:

> *Where is another God like you, who pardons the sins of the survivors among his people? You cannot stay angry with your people forever, because you delight in showing mercy.*

One image of God pictures him as judge and emphasizes his anger—as the righteous Sovereign, he judges sin and punishes sinners. Certainly this picture is true; God does reign supreme and just. And we should fear his wrath and obey his commands. This verse in Micah, however, emphasizes that God does not stay angry forever. In fact, God *delights* in showing mercy.

In this image, God is like a loving father with a disobedient child. Knowing that he must punish, he would much rather have the child repent so that he can show mercy and forgive.

The phrase "survivors among his people" refers to God's true children—people of faith. That's you, if you have trusted Christ as Savior.

So hear the lesson: Your Father loves you and stands ready to show you mercy and pardon your sin. Don't be afraid. Don't run away in fear. Confess your sin and receive his grace.

FOR FURTHER STUDY
- God's mercy is plentiful (Psalm 69:16). *page 465*
- God's mercy is unparalleled (Isaiah 63:9). *page 575*
- Even those late in coming will receive mercy (Matthew 20:1-16). *pages 747-748*
- Jesus had mercy on sinners, even in death (Luke 23:32-43). *page 810*
- God shows mercy to those he chooses (Romans 9:15). *page 872*

- No one can earn God's mercy (Romans 9:16). *page 872*
- God offers his mercy (2 Timothy 1:2). *page 928*
- God saves because of his mercy (Titus 3:5). *page 932*

to OBEY GOD

Sometimes you may wonder if obeying God is worth it. Job's friend, Elihu, concluded in Job 36:11 that God is just and does bless those who obey him. If you don't reap the benefits of obedience in this life, you will in the next.

> *"If they listen and obey God, then they will be blessed with prosperity throughout their lives. All their years will be pleasant."*

The Pharisees in Jesus' day obeyed the law, but for all the wrong reasons. Jesus warned in Matthew 5:20 that God looks at people's hearts. He wants obedience that flows out of love for him.

> *"But I warn you—unless you obey God better than the teachers of religious law and the Pharisees do, you can't enter the Kingdom of Heaven at all!"*

When the religious leaders commanded Peter and the apostles to stop preaching the gospel, their priorities were put to the test. Their answer, recorded in Acts 5:29, teaches us that obedience to God must come first, even if it requires personal sacrifice.

> But Peter and the apostles replied, "We must obey
> God rather than human authority."

God has not hidden the secret of obedience—he
has made his expectations clear. Micah 6:8
summarizes the way people can please God.

> No, O people, the LORD has already told you what
> is good, and this is what he requires: to do what is
> right, to love mercy, and to walk humbly with
> your God.

At times, you may wonder what God expects.
With the multitude of churches and wide variety
of religious voices added to the messages from
your personal study and your conscience, you may
feel overwhelmed with duties and obligations. In
a simple statement, however, the prophet Micah
gives clear direction: (1) *do what is right*, (2) *love
mercy*, (3) *walk humbly*.

Justice. Mercy. Humility. Consider the difference
those qualities can make if consistently applied.
How would your life change? What would be the
impact on your relationships? What would your
community and nation be like if citizens lived
according to this pattern? Most important, what
would happen in your relationship with God?

In reality, the application of those changes in
behavior occurs in the reverse order. First, we
must humble ourselves before God, giving our
total allegiance to him. Next, we must relate to
others with mercy, loving and caring for our
neighbors. Then, this genuine care will lead to
standing for what is right in society and fighting
against sin and injustice.

This summary in Micah reveals what God wants
from you. They are the key to obedience.

FOR FURTHER STUDY
• Obeying is better than saying, "I'm sorry" (1 Samuel 15:22).
  page 233
• People who obey God's Word will be blessed (Luke 11:28).
  page 795
• Christians should obey the government (Romans 13:1-4).
  page 875
• Children should obey their parents (Ephesians 6:1). *page 910*
• Christians obey God (1 John 2:3). *page 956*

for PATIENCE

David had learned from many years of difficulties what it meant to wait patiently for the Lord. When enemies surrounded him, he reminded himself again to *wait* on God for his deliverance. He wrote in Psalm 27:14:

> *Wait patiently for the LORD. Be brave and coura-geous. Yes, wait patiently for the LORD.*

Patience does not come naturally to most people. Galatians 5:22-23 tells us it is a gift from the Holy Spirit.

> *But when the Holy Spirit controls our lives, he will produce this kind of fruit in us: love, joy, peace, patience, kindness, goodness, faithfulness, gentle-ness, and self-control. Here there is no conflict with the law.*

God *wants* us to endure, so he *will* give us all the patience we need! Paul prayed this for his fellow

141

believers in Colosse, just as we should pray for patience for one another. Colossians 1:11 gives us the words to pray:

> We also pray that you will be strengthened with his glorious power so that you will have all the patience and endurance you need.

Waiting is difficult in a hurried, fast-paced world. Waiting is frustrating for impatient people. We want answers and service and money and success and healing . . . NOW!

But God says to have patience, to wait for him and *his* timing.

That makes sense, of course. God knows us, he knows the future, and his timing is perfect. Of course we should wait. Of course we should endure. Of course we should listen for his voice and follow his guidance.

Instead, we rush headlong into life. Then we wonder why we struggle and fear.

Waiting for the Lord means recognizing his wisdom, admitting his sovereignty, and submitting to his control. Waiting involves prayer, talking to God about our dilemmas and decisions, and pouring out our feelings. But as we wait, God gives us strength and courage to meet the challenges before us.

Looking for a quick fix? Immediate gratification? Easy answers? Instead, wait for the Lord and ask him to give you the patience you need.

FOR FURTHER STUDY
- Patience is valuable (Proverbs 25:15). *page 521*
- Patience is better than pride (Ecclesiastes 7:8). *page 529*
- Patience demonstrates love (1 Corinthians 13:4). *page 888*
- Christians are to be patient with each other (Ephesians 4:2). *page 909*

- God wants to clothe us with patience (Colossians 3:12). *page 918*
- We can be examples of God's great patience (1 Timothy 1:16). *page 924*

for PEACE

God gave Aaron and his sons this special blessing to pronounce on the people of Israel to remind them of God's care for them. This blessing, recorded in Numbers 6:24-26, shows that God *wants* to give us his peace, we simply must receive it.

> *"May the LORD bless you and protect you. May the LORD smile on you and be gracious to you. May the LORD show you his favor and give you his peace."*

We cannot escape the concerns of this world, but we can experience God's peace in the midst of our troubles. Isaiah 26:3 is a wonderful promise for us to claim:

> *You will keep in perfect peace all who trust in you, whose thoughts are fixed on you!*

Peace is a choice. Philippians 4:6-7 tells us that we will experience God's peace when we trust him with all of our needs.

> *Don't worry about anything; instead, pray about everything. Tell God what you need, and thank*

*him for all he has done. If you do this, you will
experience God's peace, which is far more wonderful than the human mind can understand. His
peace will guard your hearts and minds as you live
in Christ Jesus.*

David must have often feared for his safety as he
encountered enemies at every turn, but he learned
how to allow God's peace to flow over him and
fill him, so that he could rest secure in God's
loving arms. He wrote in Psalm 4:8:

*I will lie down in peace and sleep, for you alone,
O LORD, will keep me safe.*

For months, David had been harassed in the
palace and then chased through the desert by King
Saul. Later, during his own reign as king, David
faced a host of enemies, both from outside Israel's
borders and from within. Eventually, even his
own sons Absalom and Adonijah tried to over-
throw him. He could have been paralyzed with
fear. But instead, David was filled with peace,
confident in his relationship with his loving heavenly Father. He wrote that he could "lie down in
peace and sleep" because he knew God would
protect him.

You, like David, may be surrounded by enemies
who are intent on causing you great harm.
Perhaps even loved ones have turned against you.
And, if you're honest, you might have to admit
that sleep has not come easily at night, with anxi-
eties and fears filling your dreams. You may even
fear for your life.

If so, check out David's cure for insomnia—his
recipe for sleeping "in peace." The secret? David
focused his attention on his Lord instead of on his

situation, remembering God's power and love. And he prayed about his circumstances and his worries.

David knew that lasting peace comes from God alone.

FOR FURTHER STUDY
- Peace is a blessing from God (Psalm 29:11). *page 444*
- Jesus is known as the Prince of Peace (Isaiah 9:6-7). *page 542*
- You can have peace with God (Isaiah 53:5). *page 570*
- The peace Jesus offers is different than the world's peace (John 14:27). *page 828*
- Jesus gives peace (Romans 5:1). *page 868*
- Peace comes from believing in God (Romans 15:13). *page 877*
- Peace is evidence of the Holy Spirit's work (Galatians 5:22). *page 906*

to resist PEER PRESSURE

Peer pressure can push us to conform to wrong values. Exodus 23:2 encourages us to stand strong against pressure to do wrong.

"Do not join a crowd that intends to do evil. When you are on the witness stand, do not be swayed in your testimony by the opinion of the majority."

The people of Israel were surrounded by pagan people who worshiped idols. They often gave in to worldly pressures which brought God's judgment down on them. Judges 2:11-14 warns God's people of the consequences of succumbing to peer pressure.

> Then the Israelites did what was evil in the LORD's sight and worshiped the images of Baal. They abandoned the LORD, the God of their ancestors, who had brought them out of Egypt. They chased after other gods, worshiping the gods of the people around them. And they angered the LORD. They abandoned the LORD to serve Baal and the images of Ashtoreth. This made the LORD burn with anger against Israel, so he handed them over to marauders who stole their possessions. He sold them to their enemies all around, and they were no longer able to resist them.

Second Thessalonians 3:6-7 tells us we can resist peer pressure by avoiding the people and things that tempt us to sin.

> And now, dear brothers and sisters, we give you this command with the authority of our Lord Jesus Christ: Stay away from any Christian who lives in idleness and doesn't follow the tradition of hard work we gave you. For you know that you ought to follow our example. We were never lazy when we were with you.

FOR FURTHER STUDY
- Sometimes it is necessary to speak up against the majority (Numbers 13:30-32). *page 121*
- Resisting peer pressure requires courage and self-sacrifice (Esther 3:2). *page 406*
- Your character is revealed under pressure (Proverbs 24:10). *page 520*
- Obey and serve God regardless of what others think (2 Corinthians 6:8). *page 896*

for God's PERSPECTIVE

Without God's perspective, we can lose hope and get discouraged. Luke 18:27 declares that all things are possible with God—we should look at our problems from God's perspective.

> *[Jesus] replied, "What is impossible from a human perspective is possible with God."*

God is not elusive—he reveals himself in his Word. First John 2:5 tells us that we can discover God's perspective in the Bible.

> *But those who obey God's word really do love him. That is the way to know whether or not we live in him.*

FOR FURTHER STUDY
- God's perspective is greater than yours (Exodus 4:10-13). *page 48*
- Understanding God's perspective brings hope (Leviticus 26:40-45). *pages 106-107*
- You can lose your perspective by focusing on your problems instead of focusing on God (Numbers 16:13-14). *page 124*
- You can learn God's perspective through prayer (Psalm 13:1-6). *page 436*
- God's perspective differs from human opinion (Matthew 16:23). *page 745*
- God's perspective helps you do what is important in life (Matthew 16:26). *page 745*

- Contentment comes from seeing from God's perspective (Philippians 4:12-13). *pages 914-915*

for PHYSICAL HEALING

In Isaiah 57:18-19, the Lord offers hope and healing to the people of Judah, despite their unfaithfulness.

> *"I have seen what they do, but I will heal them anyway! I will lead them and comfort those who mourn. Then words of praise will be on their lips. May they have peace, both near and far, for I will heal them all," says the LORD.*

James 5:13-16 highlights the importance of praying in faith and turning to other believers for support when we are in need of physical healing.

> *Are any among you suffering? They should keep on praying about it. And those who have reason to be thankful should continually sing praises to the Lord. Are any among you sick? They should call for the elders of the church and have them pray over them, anointing them with oil in the name of the Lord. And their prayer offered in faith will heal the sick, and the Lord will make them well. And anyone who has committed sins will be forgiven. Confess your sins to each other and pray for each other so that you may be healed. The earnest prayer of a righteous person has great power and wonderful results.*

- Medicines can be helpful in healing (2 Kings 20:7). *page 318*
- Obeying God's law can bring healing (Psalm 119:93). *page 494*
- Laughter can help bring healing (Proverbs 17:22). *page 516*
- God's discipline can be a means to healing (Isaiah 38:16). *page 560*
- Christ suffered for your ultimate healing (Isaiah 53:5). *page 570*
- The faith of friends can bring healing (Mark 2:1-5). *page 761*
- God has the power to miraculously heal (Mark 3:1-5). *page 762*
- God can heal from spiritual oppression (Mark 5:1-20). *page 764*
- Faith is important in God's work of healing (Luke 5:12-16). *page 786*
- Exercise is helpful for maintaining health (1 Timothy 4:8). *page 925*

for POPULARITY

Haman relished his popularity and the power of his position. When Mordecai refused to give him the respect he thought he deserved, he was furious. His story in Esther 3:5 warns of the dangers of seeking popularity and finding self-worth in other people's opinions.

> *When Haman saw that Mordecai would not bow*
> *down or show him respect, he was filled with rage.*

There were many false prophets in Old Testament times who sought popularity over the truth. Telling people what they want to hear may make a person popular, but it doesn't last. Jesus warns us in Luke 6:26 that we will be disappointed if we seek the praise of people rather than God's approval.

> *"What sorrows await you who are praised by*
> *the crowds, for their ancestors also praised false*
> *prophets."*

God doesn't promise popularity to those who follow him, but he does provide his presence. In 2 Timothy 2:9, Paul described what he had to give up to preach the gospel.

> *And because I preach this Good News, I am*
> *suffering and have been chained like a criminal.*
> *But the word of God cannot be chained.*

FOR FURTHER STUDY
- People can lust for popularity (Esther 6:7-9). *page 408*
- The Christian life is not a popularity contest (Matthew 9:11-12). *page 736*
- Avoid being jealous over other's popularity (John 3:26). *page 814*
- Popularity brings only temporary commitment (John 12:18). *page 825*
- You may have to sacrifice popularity for your faith (1 John 4:6). *page 958*

for POWER

God gives power to his people when they obey him. In Deuteronomy 20:3-4, God promised to give the Israelites power to overcome their enemies because that was his plan. They didn't need to fear because God was on their side!

He will say, "Listen to me, all you men of Israel! Do not be afraid as you go out to fight today! Do not lose heart or panic. For the LORD your God is going with you! He will fight for you against your enemies, and he will give you victory!"

When David's army suffered defeat at the hands of their enemies, David turned to God for help. He knew he was powerless without God's help and protection. So David reaffirmed his faith in God, declaring in Psalm 60:12:

With God's help we will do mighty things, for he will trample down our foes.

God loves to show his strength in our weakness. When we feel helpless, God can demonstrate his power through us. Isaiah 40:29 promises:

He gives power to those who are tired and worn out; he offers strength to the weak.

Throughout the Old Testament, God promised the Israelites that he would be with them and give them power to defeat their foes. Regardless of the enemy, God's people did not need to fear, because God would fight with them and for them, assuring them of victory.

Enemies continue to threaten God's people: financial struggles, failing health, job stress, family conflict, persecution. Normal reactions to such daunting battles include frustration, fear, and, often, outright terror. Instead, God tells us to recall his previous work—past assurances of his presence and demonstrations of his power—and to know that this same powerful God is with us *today*, in *this* battle.

What enemy do you face? Don't panic. God is still all-powerful, and he loves you. God brought you through before, and he will do it again. He stands on your side, fighting for you and with you.

Know who marches with you, and move forward in his power. He will help you overcome!

FOR FURTHER STUDY
- You can experience God's power through faith (Mark 11:20-25). *page 772*
- Christians receive power from the Holy Spirit (Acts 1:8). *page 835*
- The Holy Spirit gives power to change (Romans 8:1-14). *pages 870-871*
- The Bible is a powerful weapon (Ephesians 6:17). *page 911*
- Jesus' power is greater than any other power (Hebrews 1:1-4). *page 934*
- Christians have power to overcome the world (1 John 5:4-5). *page 958*

to PRAISE GOD

God is the Creator of the universe, our Savior and our Lord—he deserves our best praise! Psalm 33:2-3 admonishes God's people to use their musical and creative abilities to offer quality praise to God.

> *Praise the LORD with melodies on the lyre; make music for him on the ten-stringed harp. Sing new songs of praise to him; play skillfully on the harp and sing with joy.*

Isaiah wrote a hymn of praise to God describing the people's joy in God's deliverance. Isaiah 12:1-2 reminds us to express our gratitude to God for all he does for us.

> *In that day you will sing: "Praise the LORD! He was angry with me, but now he comforts me. See, God has come to save me. I will trust in him and not be afraid. The LORD GOD is my strength and my song; he has become my salvation."*

We can offer God our praise anytime and anywhere. Hebrews 13:15 tells us that God receives our acts of obedience and service as praise to him.

> *With Jesus' help, let us continually offer our sacrifice of praise to God by proclaiming the glory of his name.*

FOR FURTHER STUDY
- Praise should be a continuous part of life (1 Chronicles 16:4). *page 339*
- Worship should begin with praise (2 Chronicles 5:13). *page 355*
- God deserves your praise (Ezra 3:10-11). *page 384*
- Praise God daily (Psalm 61:8). *page 461*
- Praise should be part of your prayers (Luke 11:1-4). *page 795*
- Praise God despite your circumstances (Acts 16:22-25). *page 852*

for answers to PRAYER

We don't know the nature of the struggle David faced before he heard from God. The words in Psalm 40:1-2 indicate that his situation was extremely unpleasant. Yet David waited patiently for the Lord and trusted that God would answer his prayer.

> *I waited patiently for the LORD to help me, and he turned to me and heard my cry. He lifted me out of the pit of despair, out of the mud and the mire. He set my feet on solid ground and steadied me as I walked along.*

Micah rebuked the leaders and prophets of Israel for their rebellion against God. His stern warning to them in Micah 3:4 reminds us that God does not answer the prayers of unrepentant people.

> *Then you beg the LORD for help in times of trouble! Do you really expect him to listen? After all the evil you have done, he won't even look at you!*

In contrast to Micah 3:4, Proverbs 15:29 reveals that God does hear the prayers of righteous people. He loves to answer our prayers when we live in obedience to him.

> *The LORD is far from the wicked, but he hears the prayers of the righteous.*

Waiting for answers to prayer takes patience, especially when we need help immediately. And pain, problems, and pressures increase the difficulty—minutes can seem like days and hours like weeks. But, like David, our patient reliance on God will be rewarded.

Often God wants to teach us during those difficult times of waiting for answers, solutions, and resolutions. He wants us to learn that *he* is in control and that *he* alone is our sure foundation and ally.

Are you waiting for God's touch? For his answers? For his rescue? Keep crying for help, but in your cries, be patient. He will give you the answers you need at the times you need them.

FOR FURTHER STUDY
- God may not answer your prayers the way you want (Job 42:1-3). *page 431*
- Prayer should not be a show (Matthew 6:6). *page 733*
- Jesus taught his disciples how to pray (Matthew 6:9-13). *page 733*
- Pray with an attitude of humility (Luke 18:9-14). *page 803*
- Pray in Jesus' name (John 16:23-24). *page 829*
- Pray all the time (Ephesians 6:18). *page 911*
- Pray without doubting (James 1:6). *page 945*
- Pray with the right motives (James 4:3). *page 947*
- Pray according to God's will (1 John 5:14-15). *page 959*

for help in setting PRIORITIES

The people of Judah had not given God first place in their lives; as a result, God did not give them success or fulfillment. Haggai 1:8-9 describes their confused priorities.

> Now go up into the hills, bring down timber, and rebuild my house. Then I will take pleasure in it and be honored, says the LORD. You hoped for rich harvests, but they were poor. And when you brought your harvest home, I blew it away. Why? Because my house lies in ruins, says the LORD Almighty, while you are all busy building your own fine houses.

We can determine our priorities by looking at what occupies our thoughts, time, and energy. Jesus warns us in Matthew 6:24 that we can become preoccupied with wealth, giving it a higher place of priority than spiritual things.

> "No one can serve two masters. For you will hate one and love the other, or be devoted to one and despise the other. You cannot serve both God and money."

FOR FURTHER STUDY

- Giving reveals a person's priorities (Deuteronomy 17:1). *page 160*
- Right priorities help other things fall into proper place (2 Chronicles 1:11-12). *page 352*

- Christians should give God's Kingdom first place in their life (Matthew 6:33). *page 734*
- Following Jesus should come before any other concerns in life (Matthew 8:21-22). *page 735*
- Your priorities indicate the sincerity of your faith (Titus 1:16). *page 931*

for help in dealing with
PROBLEMS

In Matthew 9:36, Jesus demonstrated deep compassion for people's problems. He also has compassion on us—he wants us to come to him for help with our problems.

> *He felt great pity for the crowds that came, because their problems were so great and they didn't know where to go for help. They were like sheep without a shepherd.*

God never promises to rescue us from our problems, but he can use them for good in our lives. Paul encourages us in Romans 5:3 to welcome problems and rejoice when we face trials because of the way they help us grow.

> *We can rejoice, too, when we run into problems and trials, for we know that they are good for us— they help us learn to endure.*

We should not be surprised or even disappointed when we encounter difficulties. First Peter 4:12-13 encourages us to view our problems as opportunities to share in Christ's suffering.

> *Dear friends, don't be surprised at the fiery trials you are going through, as if something strange were happening to you. Instead, be very glad—because these trials will make you partners with Christ in his suffering, and afterward you will have the wonderful joy of sharing his glory when it is displayed to all the world.*

FOR FURTHER STUDY

- Problems test your faith (Genesis 12:10). *page 10*
- Do not try to solve problems by compromising what is right (Genesis 16:3). *page 12*
- Following God may bring more problems (Exodus 5:4-9). *page 49*
- Trust God with all of your problems (Numbers 14:5-9). *page 122*
- Turn to God when problems arise (Judges 4:3). *page 201*
- Problems may be a sign of effective living (1 Thessalonians 3:1-3). *page 923*
- All problems will end in eternity (Revelation 7:17). *page 968*

for PROTECTION

Johanan and his army officials asked the prophet Jeremiah for guidance from God, but they had no intention of following it. Although they wanted God's protection, they were not willing to obey him. We learn from their experience that God protects those who obey him, but removes his presence from those who rebel against him. Jeremiah 42:7-10 and 43:2 tell part of their story:

> Ten days later, the LORD gave his reply to Jeremiah. So he called for Johanan son of Kareah and the army officers, and for all the people, from the least to the greatest. He said to them, "You sent me to the LORD, the God of Israel, with your request, and this is his reply: 'Stay here in this land. If you do, I will build you up and not tear you down; I will plant you and not uproot you. For I am sorry for all the punishment I have had to bring upon you.'" Azariah son of Hoshaiah and Johanan son of Kareah and all the other proud men said to Jeremiah, "You lie! The LORD our God hasn't forbidden us to go to Egypt!

When God delivered David from all his enemies—including King Saul—David praised God for his deliverance. David gave God credit in 2 Samuel 22:3 for protecting him from his enemies.

> My God is my rock, in whom I find protection. He is my shield, the strength of my salvation, and my stronghold, my high tower, my savior, the one who saves me from violence.

Although God will not save us from our troubles, he will protect us in the midst of them. In Psalm 91:4, the psalm writer encourages us to put our faith in God's protection.

> He will shield you with his wings. He will shelter you with his feathers. His faithful promises are your armor and protection.

FOR FURTHER STUDY
• God protects those who look to him (2 Samuel 22:31). *page 266*

- God is a refuge in times of trouble (Psalm 9:9). *page 435*
- God is your protector (Psalm 18:2). *page 438*
- God himself watches over you (Psalm 121:8). *page 496*
- God protects those who fear him (Proverbs 19:23). *page 517*
- God guards you from the evil one (2 Thessalonians 3:3). *page 923*

for a PURE HEART

Solomon advises us in Proverbs 4:23 to guard our hearts because it determines how we act.

Above all else, guard your heart, for it affects everything you do.

Purity is worth pursuing—God blesses and reveals himself to those who keep their hearts pure. Matthew 5:8 is a great promise we can claim:

"God blesses those whose hearts are pure, for they will see God."

Second Timothy 2:21-22 encourages us to stay pure so that God can use us. The friendship of other mature believers can help us remain pure.

If you keep yourself pure, you will be a utensil God can use for his purpose. Your life will be clean, and you will be ready for the Master to use you for every good work. Run from anything that stimulates youthful lust. Follow anything that makes you want to do right. Pursue faith and love and peace, and enjoy the companionship of those who call on the Lord with pure hearts.

FOR FURTHER STUDY
- Only God can make you pure (Psalm 51:1-10). *page 456*
- God's Word gives instructions for living a pure life (Psalm 119:9-20). *pages 492-493*
- No one can claim purity apart from God (Proverbs 20:9). *page 518*
- Outward purity cannot substitute for inner purity (Matthew 23:25-28). *pages 751-752*
- Words and actions begin in the heart (Luke 6:45). *page 788*
- Purity comes from God (John 17:17). *page 830*
- Purity ought to mark believers' lives (Ephesians 5:1-4). *pages 909-910*
- Think about things that are pure (Philippians 4:8). *page 914*
- One day your purity will be like Christ's (1 John 3:1-3). *page 957*

for PURITY

The psalm writer posed a question that all believers should ask: How can we remain pure when we live in a filthy environment? The answer is found in Psalm 119:9:

How can a young person stay pure? By obeying your word and following its rules.

Jesus acknowledged the fact that he was leaving his disciples in a tempting environment, a place where evil threatened to overcome them. But he trusted that God would protect his followers from evil and keep them pure through the power of his word. John 17:15-17 says:

"I'm not asking you to take them out of the world, but to keep them safe from the evil one. They are not part of this world any more than I am. Make them pure and holy by teaching them your words of truth."

Thoughts lead to actions. Thus, the first step in remaining pure is to focus our thoughts on things that are true. Philippians 4:8 is a powerful reminder to believers:

And now, dear brothers and sisters, let me say one more thing as I close this letter. Fix your thoughts on what is true and honorable and right. Think about things that are pure and lovely and admirable. Think about things that are excellent and worthy of praise.

The world is filled with impurity. Temptation surrounds us, and at every turn we see new ways to disobey God, new paths that lead to sin. We desperately need to know how to stay pure.

The first truth that must sink into our minds is the fact that we cannot remain pure on our own. We are weak to temptation. We are prone to sin. We are in over our heads.

The second truth is that God can and *will* help us. His power is greater than the temptations that surround us. His strength in us can help us resist and overcome evil. How? God's Word is our best defense.

The only way to remain pure is to saturate our minds with God's Word. We claim God's strength and power by reading his word and obeying it.

FOR FURTHER STUDY
- Only God can purify someone's heart (Psalm 86:11). *page 475*
- No one can be pure apart from God (Proverbs 20:9). *page 518*
- The pure in heart will see God (Matthew 5:8). *page 732*
- Purity begins in the heart (Matthew 5:27-30). *pages 732-733*
- Outward purity cannot substitute for inner purity (Matthew 23:25-28). *pages 751-752*
- Inner purity is essential to outward purity (Mark 7:1-23). *pages 766-767*
- Purity ought to mark our lives (Ephesians 5:1-4). *pages 909-910*

for RECOGNITION

Jesus condemned the Pharisees for seeking recognition from people while not caring about pleasing God. Jesus' words in Luke 20:46 teach us that recognition is meaningless if we do not have God's approval.

"Beware of these teachers of religious law! For they love to parade in flowing robes and to have everyone bow to them as they walk in the marketplaces. And how they love the seats of honor in the synagogues and at banquets."

In John 7:18, Jesus warns us to watch out for spiritual leaders who seek honor for themselves—their message will bring attention to them, instead of

God, and may contradict God's Word. We should listen only to those who seek to honor God by preaching the truth.

"Those who present their own ideas are looking for praise for themselves, but those who seek to honor the one who sent them are good and genuine."

FOR FURTHER STUDY
- God's recognition is all that matters (1 Chronicles 29:12). *page 351*
- God's recognition brings comfort (Psalm 71:21). *page 466*
- Wise people receive recognition; fools are shamed (Proverbs 3:35). *page 508*
- Earthly recognition fades quickly (Ecclesiastes 6:2). *page 528*
- Striving for recognition is dangerous (Luke 11:43). *page 796*

for RECONCILIATION

Proverbs 14:9 teaches that it is foolish to refuse to make amends with people; wise people are eager to make things right with others.

Fools make fun of guilt, but the godly acknowledge it and seek reconciliation.

The last scene of the parable of the prodigal or lost son recorded in Luke 15:20-24 is a beautiful picture of reconciliation. It offers hope to everyone who has strayed from home or rebelled against the Father.

"So [the son] returned home to his father. And while he was still a long distance away, his father

saw him coming. Filled with love and compassion, he ran to his son, embraced him, and kissed him. His son said to him, 'Father, I have sinned against both heaven and you, and I am no longer worthy of being called your son.'

"But his father said to the servants, 'Quick! Bring the finest robe in the house and put it on him. Get a ring for his finger, and sandals for his feet. And kill the calf we have been fattening in the pen. We must celebrate with a feast, for this son of mine was dead and has now returned to life. He was lost, but now he is found.' So the party began."

In the happy ending to Jesus' marvelous parable, the father runs to his prodigal son, welcoming him home. Note that the father sees the son "while he was still a long distance away"; thus, he must have been looking daily for his wayward boy. And when he catches a glimpse of the bedraggled and contrite young man in the distance, the father drops everything and runs to his beloved son. Nothing is more important than this homecoming, this joyous reunion.

The father represents God—loving, giving, and patiently waiting. And we, his wayward children, are represented by the son.

Where are you in the story? Perhaps you are ready to leave home—tired of the restrictions and rules, you want to go your own way. Maybe you are in the "distant land" (Luke 15:13), far from home and having a ball. Perhaps you are in the pigpen—broke, hungry, and painfully aware of what you left behind. Maybe you're headed back, rehearsing your speech of repentance. Or you may be in between those points in the story.

Wherever you are, your loving Father waits for your return. Standing at the edge of the yard, peering into the distance, he looks for that familiar form. "Filled with love and compassion," he is ready to run, to open his arms and welcome you back, to hug and kiss you, to be reconciled with you, and to celebrate your return.

FOR FURTHER STUDY
- Believers should make things right with others before approaching God (Matthew 5:24). *page 764*
- God wants you to be reconciled to him (2 Corinthians 5:20). *page 896*
- Reconciliation comes through God alone (Colossians 1:20). *page 916*

for good RELATIONSHIPS

When it comes to relationships, it's wise to treat others the way we would like to be treated—with humility, generosity, and forgiveness. Jesus gives helpful advice in Luke 6:37-38 about how to maintain good relationships.

> *"Stop judging others, and you will not be judged. Stop criticizing others, or it will all come back on you. If you forgive others, you will be forgiven. If you give, you will receive. Your gift will return to you in full measure, pressed down, shaken together to make room for more, and running over. Whatever measure you use in giving—large*

or small—it will be used to measure what is given back to you."

Relationships are deepened when friends help one another through difficult times. We can strengthen our relationships by extending the care and comfort we've received from God to our friends. Paul reminds us of this in 2 Corinthians 1:3-4:

All praise to the God and Father of our Lord Jesus Christ. He is the source of every mercy and the God who comforts us. He comforts us in all our troubles so that we can comfort others. When others are troubled, we will be able to give them the same comfort God has given us.

Ephesians 6:1-5 is filled with practical advice about relationships. Our relationships with family, friends, and employers often indicate the depth of our faith. If we want to please God, we will work hard to maintain good relationships.

Children, obey your parents because you belong to the Lord, for this is the right thing to do. "Honor your father and mother." This is the first of the Ten Commandments that ends with a promise. And this is the promise: If you honor your father and mother, "you will live a long life, full of blessing." And now a word to you fathers. Don't make your children angry by the way you treat them. Rather, bring them up with the discipline and instruction approved by the Lord. Slaves, obey your earthly masters with deep respect and fear. Serve them sincerely as you would serve Christ.

FOR FURTHER STUDY
• Relationships can be built through hospitality (Genesis 18:2-5). *pages 13-14*

for a good REPUTATION

The best way to gain a good reputation is to focus on obeying God, not earning the approval of others. Proverbs 3:3-4 tells us that people who honor God often win the respect of others.

Never let loyalty and kindness get away from you! Wear them like a necklace; write them deep within your heart. Then you will find favor with both God and people, and you will gain a good reputation.

Proverbs 22:1 speaks of the value of a good reputation. Guard your reputation—if you lose it, it's difficult to regain.

Choose a good reputation over great riches, for

being held in high esteem is better than having silver or gold.

FOR FURTHER STUDY

- A good reputation can be built by obeying God's Word (Deuteronomy 4:5-14). *page 149*
- Integrity builds a good reputation (Ruth 2:1-13). *pages 218-219*
- A bad reputation will follow you (Proverbs 25:9-10). *page 521*
- The Christians in Rome had a reputation for obedience (Romans 16:19). *page 878*
- Guard your reputation (2 Corinthians 8:18-24). *pages 897-898*
- Maintain a good reputation among non-Christians (Colossians 4:5). *page 918*

for RESPECT

When God appeared to Moses through a burning bush, Moses was overcome by God's brilliance and holiness. God is holy and just—he deserves our highest respect. Exodus 3:4-6 describes Moses' encounter with God:

When the LORD saw that he had caught Moses' attention, God called to him from the bush, "Moses! Moses!" "Here I am!" Moses replied. "Do not come any closer," God told him. "Take off your sandals, for you are standing on holy ground." Then he said, "I am the God of your ancestors—the God of Abraham, the God of

Isaac, and the God of Jacob." When Moses heard this, he hid his face in his hands because he was afraid to look at God.

A good way to gain the respect of others is to treat them with respect. First Peter 2:17 admonishes believers to fear God and show respect for people.

Show respect for everyone. Love your Christian brothers and sisters. Fear God. Show respect for the king.

FOR FURTHER STUDY

- Your parents are worthy of respect (Leviticus 19:3). *page 98*
- Those in authority should have your respect (1 Samuel 24:1-6). *page 241*
- Do not confuse respectability with righteousness (Luke 5:30-32). *page 787*
- Husbands and wives should respect each other (Ephesians 5:33). *page 910*
- Those in leadership should have respectful children (1 Timothy 3:4). *page 925*

for RESPONSIBILITY

Luke 16:10 explains how God determines our readiness for responsibility. Jesus says that if we prove ourselves faithful in the small things, God will trust us with greater responsibilities.

"Unless you are faithful in small matters, you won't be faithful in large ones. If you cheat even a little, you won't be honest with greater responsibilities."

Romans 12:8 encourages us to take the responsibilities God gives us seriously. We should do our best to use our abilities for God's glory.

> *If your gift is to encourage others, do it! If you have money, share it generously. If God has given you leadership ability, take the responsibility seriously. And if you have a gift for showing kindness to others, do it gladly.*

FOR FURTHER STUDY

- Responsible people admit their wrongs (1 Chronicles 21:8). *page 343*
- Responsible people are faithful with what they have been given (Matthew 25:14-30). *pages 753-754*
- People are responsible for their decision about Christ (John 3:18-19). *page 814*
- Responsible people know their abilities and limitations (Acts 6:1-7). *page 840*
- You are responsible to stand up for the truth (2 Corinthians 13:8). *page 901*
- Church leaders are responsible to build up God's people (Ephesians 4:11-12). *page 909*
- It is good to desire responsibilities in the church (1 Timothy 3:1). *page 925*
- People are responsible for their own actions (James 1:13-15). *page 945*

for | REST |

God knows we need rest; he also knows we often resist giving ourselves the rest we need. In his wisdom, God declared a day of rest and modeled it himself! Exodus 20:9-11 says:

> *"Six days a week are set apart for your daily duties and regular work, but the seventh day is a day of rest dedicated to the LORD your God. On that day no one in your household may do any kind of work. This includes you, your sons and daughters, your male and female servants, your livestock, and any foreigners living among you. For in six days the LORD made the heavens, the earth, the sea, and everything in them; then he rested on the seventh day. That is why the LORD blessed the Sabbath day and set it apart as holy."*

The rest Jesus promises is not necessarily a break from our labors, but it is peace, contentment, love, and healing that renew our spirits and strengthen our souls. Matthew 11:28-29 states:

> *Then Jesus said, "Come to me, all of you who are weary and carry heavy burdens, and I will give you rest. Take my yoke upon you. Let me teach you, because I am humble and gentle, and you will find rest for your souls."*

David accepted rest as a gift from his Good Shepherd. Psalm 23:1-3 expresses David's appreciation of God's good care for him:

> *The LORD is my shepherd; I have everything I need. He lets me rest in green meadows; he leads me beside peaceful streams. He renews my strength. He guides me along right paths, bringing honor to his name.*

When trials and time join forces to ravage us, tearing at body and mind and crushing the spirit, we desperately need rest—to be refreshed and renewed.

But only the Lord can do that work. As our original designer and creator, only he knows us and our unique needs. Only he can restore our souls.

God begins this miracle of restoration by leading us, like a caring shepherd, away from the bustle and traffic, stress and storms, to the green meadows where we can rest and eat. And he leads us to the peaceful streams, the still waters—calm, quiet, deep, inviting—where we can quench our thirst and receive his loving care.

Renewal begins when we, like frightened sheep, stop running and struggling and submit to our Shepherd. God wants to restore our souls, and he has everything we need.

FOR FURTHER STUDY
- God gave an example and a command to rest (Genesis 2:1-3). *page 3*
- God offers rest and shelter to his people (Psalm 91:1). *page 478*
- God gives the Sabbath as a day of rest (Isaiah 56:6). *pages 571-572*
- Rest is a gift from God (Hebrews 4:9-11). *page 936*
- Heaven will be a place of rest (Revelation 14:13). *page 972*

for RESURRECTION

Through his death and resurrection, Jesus conquered sin and has power over life and death. If we receive Jesus as the Life-giver, we will be raised with him. Jesus declared this truth in John 11:25-26:

> *Jesus told her, "I am the resurrection and the life. Those who believe in me, even though they die like everyone else, will live again. They are given eternal life for believing in me and will never perish."*

Faith in Jesus gives us new life now and the hope of resurrection in the future. God gives us this promise in Romans 6:4-5:

> *For we died and were buried with Christ by baptism. And just as Christ was raised from the dead by the glorious power of the Father, now we also may live new lives. Since we have been united with him in his death, we will also be raised as he was.*

FOR FURTHER STUDY
- Christ's resurrection is a historical fact (Matthew 28:5-10). *page 758*
- All people will be resurrected (John 5:24-30). *page 816*
- Jesus promised to raise his followers (John 6:38-40). *page 818*
- Christians are dead to sin and raised to new life in Christ (Romans 6:3-11). *page 869*
- Jesus' resurrection is the foundation of Christianity (1 Corinthians 15:12-21). *page 890*
- Your resurrected body will be eternal (1 Corinthians 15:51-53). *page 891*

for REVENGE

God gives us rules to follow for our own good. He advises us in Leviticus 19:18 to love others, instead of seeking revenge or holding grudges, because he knows that is best for us.

"Never seek revenge or bear a grudge against anyone, but love your neighbor as yourself. I am the LORD."

Jesus' words in Matthew 5:39-42 are radical and challenging. He tells us that it is better to give up our rights than to demand them, and better to show mercy than to receive it. His words leave no room for revenge.

"But I say, don't resist an evil person! If you are slapped on the right cheek, turn the other, too. If you are ordered to court and your shirt is taken from you, give your coat, too. If a soldier demands that you carry his gear for a mile, carry it two miles. Give to those who ask, and don't turn away from those who want to borrow."

Romans 12:19 commands us not to seek revenge—it will only bring us more pain. We can trust God to ensure that justice prevails.

Dear friends, never avenge yourselves. Leave that to God. For it is written, "I will take vengeance; I will repay those who deserve it," says the Lord.

for RIGHTEOUSNESS

We can never attain righteousness on our own.
Philippians 3:9 tells us that only Jesus can make
us right with God.

> *I no longer count on my own goodness or my abil-*
> *ity to obey God's law, but I trust Christ to save*
> *me. For God's way of making us right with*
> *himself depends on faith.*

Second Timothy 3:16 emphasizes the power of
God's Word which teaches us the truth and helps
us do what is right. We cannot attain righteousness without obeying God's Word.

> *All Scripture is inspired by God and is useful to*
> *teach us what is true and to make us realize what*
> *is wrong in our lives. It straightens us out and*
> *teaches us to do what is right.*

- Righteousness is not attained by works (Romans 4:18-25). *page 868*
- Legalism cannot make anyone righteous (Galatians 3:11-21). *pages 903-904*
- God-given righteousness is our protection against Satan (Ephesians 6:14). *page 911*
- Christians should be characterized by righteousness (1 Peter 2:24). *page 951*

for SAFETY

Many people believe that wealth can make them safe and secure, but Proverbs 18:10-11 declares that God alone provides safety.

The name of the LORD is a strong fortress; the godly run to him and are safe. The rich think of their wealth as an impregnable defense; they imagine it is a high wall of safety.

Paul and his companions faced many dangers as they traveled to preach the gospel, so Paul asked the Corinthian believers to pray for their safety. Second Corinthians 1:11 reveals his faith that God would answer their prayers.

He will rescue us because you are helping by praying for us. As a result, many will give thanks to God because so many people's prayers for our safety have been answered.

Just before the Israelites moved into the Promised Land and just before Moses' death, Moses blessed the nation of Israel. This blessing in Deuteronomy 33:27 promises that God will keep his people safe, held securely in his "everlasting arms."

> *The eternal God is your refuge, and his everlasting arms are under you. He thrusts out the enemy before you; it is he who cries, "Destroy them!"*

Picture a muscular young shepherd carrying a frightened lamb through a storm, above swirling river waters, to the safety of the fold. The shepherd's steps are sure, and his hold on the lamb is strong.

Or picture a father lifting his child and pulling her close in a loving embrace, wiping her tears and assuring her that she is safe.

That's God—loving, strong, and always there. His "arms" hold us safely, securely, and eternally. They *never* let go.

What enemies threaten you today? What dangers surround you? No matter what your circumstances, you are safe in your Father's "everlasting arms."

FOR FURTHER STUDY
- God leads you to safety because he loves you (2 Samuel 22:20). *page 266*
- God watches over those he loves (Psalm 3:5). *page 432*
- God provides safety for his people (Psalm 18:19). *page 438*
- God alone provides safety (Psalm 91:2). *page 478*
- Safety comes to those who listen to God (Proverbs 1:33). *page 507*
- Trusting God brings safety (Proverbs 29:25). *page 523*

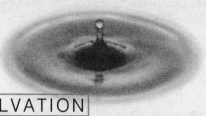

for SALVATION

The gospel message is outlined clearly in Romans 6:22-23. There is *one* way to receive forgiveness for sin and eternal life—through Jesus Christ.

> *But now you are free from the power of sin and have become slaves of God. Now you do those things that lead to holiness and result in eternal life. For the wages of sin is death, but the free gift of God is eternal life through Christ Jesus our Lord.*

God's plan of salvation for the world does not involve any striving or working on our part. Romans 10:8 explains that salvation is within our reach—it comes from simple faith in the person of Jesus.

> *Salvation that comes from trusting Christ—which is the message we preach—is already within easy reach. In fact, the Scriptures say, "The message is close at hand; it is on your lips and in your heart."*

Isaiah's prophesies about the Messiah allowed the people of Israel to look forward to the day when a Savior would come to bring forgiveness and peace. Isaiah 53:5-6 predicted that the Messiah would need to suffer to take away the sins of the world.

> *But he was wounded and crushed for our sins. He was beaten that we might have peace. He was whipped, and we were healed! All of us have strayed away like sheep. We have left God's paths*

to follow our own. Yet the LORD laid on him the
guilt and sins of us all.

Hundreds of years before Jesus' birth, Isaiah prophesied that our Lord would be wounded, crushed, beaten, and whipped. Looking back centuries later, we know that Jesus completely fulfilled all of these inspired predictions.

On the cross, Jesus took the punishment that should have been ours for our sins, bearing the scorn and pain and separation from his Father. Thus, now, because of what Christ did, we can be forgiven, know peace with God, and have eternal life. This is salvation and it is available to *you*.

FOR FURTHER STUDY
• Receiving salvation makes you God's child (John 1:12-13).
    page 812
• Salvation is a work of the Holy Spirit (John 3:1-16). *page 814*
• Trusting in Jesus Christ is the only way to be saved (John 14:6). *page 827*
• Receiving salvation means turning from sins (Acts 2:37-38).
    page 837
• Salvation is by God's grace alone (Ephesians 2:1-9). *pages 907-908*
• Salvation rescues you from Satan's dominion (Colossians 1:13-14). *page 916*
• Your salvation was obtained by Jesus' blood (1 Peter 1:18-19). *page 947*

for a SECURE FUTURE

If you love God, your future is secure. Deuteronomy 5:29 holds a beautiful promise for believers.

> *Oh, that they would always have hearts like this, that they might fear me and obey all my commands! If they did, they and their descendants would prosper forever.*

Our future is more than secure—it is greater than we can ever imagine. First Corinthians 2:9 describes the awesome things God is preparing for those who follow him.

> *That is what the Scriptures mean when they say, "No eye has seen, no ear has heard, and no mind has imagined what God has prepared for those who love him."*

FOR FURTHER STUDY
- Do not resort to pagan ways to try to discern the future (Jeremiah 10:2-3). *page 587*
- God is preparing a glorious future for those who love him (Ephesians 4:4). *page 909*

for SECURITY

Job's friend Bildad warned Job of the foolishness of trusting in anything other than God for security. Job 8:13-15 describes the consequences of trusting in worldly possessions for security.

> *Such is the fate of all who forget God. The hope of the godless comes to nothing. Everything they count on will collapse. They are leaning on a spiderweb. They cling to their home for security, but it won't last. They try to hold it fast, but it will not endure.*

God knows the best way to live. When we follow his laws, we experience the best life has to offer. Proverbs 19:23 lists security as one of the many benefits of obeying and honoring God.

> *Fear of the LORD gives life, security, and protection from harm.*

David was a warrior skilled in battle. His song of praise to God in 2 Samuel 22:2-4 uses images of war ("shield," "fortress," "stronghold") to describe the security God gives to his people.

> *"The LORD is my rock, my fortress, and my savior; my God is my rock, in whom I find protection. He is my shield, the strength of my salvation, and my stronghold, my high tower, my savior, the one who saves me from violence. I will call on the LORD, who is worthy of praise, for he saves me from my enemies."*

Toddlers clutch blankets, cloth diapers, stuffed toys, and other security symbols, dragging them wherever they go. They're cute, but that's because they're babies. Older children, teenagers, and adults with similar actions would be seen as mentally slow or emotionally weak. Yet, today, many adults tightly clutch other socially acceptable "security blankets": a special relationship, fame, good health, a prestigious career, talent, prized possessions, money. Some security! Each one of these "blankets" can be lost, stolen, or swept away, and each will fail when needed most.

In contrast, listen to the words of David as he describes his source of security: "rock," "fortress," "savior," "shield," "stronghold," "high tower." David knew from personal experience that God alone could give him the security he needed.

What are you holding? On what are you depending? Build your life on the rock—God almighty. He's the only secure foundation. He never changes. And the security he offers is eternal!

FOR FURTHER STUDY
- God's people live in security (Psalm 102:28). *page 483*
- God's presence is more enduring than mountains (Isaiah 54:10). *page 571*
- Obeying God's Word brings security (Matthew 7:24-27). *page 735*
- Nothing can separate you from God's love (Romans 8:31-39). *pages 871-872*
- Security comes through prayer (Philippians 4:6-7). *page 914*

for SELF-CONTROL

In 1 Corinthians 9:25, Paul compares the Christian life to winning a race—just like athletes need to control their bodies and impulses to win, we need to exercise self-control to gain the eternal prize we seek.

All athletes practice strict self-control. They do it to win a prize that will fade away, but we do it for an eternal prize.

The promised return of our Lord Jesus should motivate us to live carefully so we will be found faithful. First Peter 1:13 highlights the importance of living with self-control while we eagerly await Christ's return.

So think clearly and exercise self-control. Look forward to the special blessings that will come to you at the return of Jesus Christ.

Second Peter 1:6 explains the benefits of self-control—it develops character and endurance in us. Ask God to give you self-control so that your choices and actions will honor him.

Knowing God leads to self-control. Self-control leads to patient endurance, and patient endurance leads to godliness.

- Lack of self-control ends in destruction (Proverbs 5:23). *page 509*
- Self-control is shown by your ability to hold your tongue (Proverbs 13:3). *page 513*
- Self-control is more valuable than power and wealth (Proverbs 16:32). *page 516*

for SELF-WORTH

Genesis 1:27 states that God created human beings in his image—what better reason to feel positive about ourselves! Criticizing ourselves or feeling unworthy insults God and his creation.

So God created people in his own image; God patterned them after himself; male and female he created them.

David praised God in Psalm 139:13-17 for knowing him, loving him, and creating him with such care. God deserves your praise for the way he created you. You hold the image of God—don't downplay the worth you have in God's eyes.

You made all the delicate, inner parts of my body and knit me together in my mother's womb. Thank you for making me so wonderfully complex! Your workmanship is marvelous—and how well I know it. You watched me as I was being formed in utter seclusion, as I was woven together in the dark of the womb. You saw me before I was born.

*Every day of my life was recorded in your book.
Every moment was laid out before a single day
had passed. How precious are your thoughts about
me, O God! They are innumerable!*

Our true worth comes from God, not other people's opinions of us. God values and cares for us because we are his precious children. In Luke 12:6-7, Jesus encourages us to rest secure in God's love for us.

*"What is the price of five sparrows? A couple of
pennies? Yet God does not forget a single one of
them. And the very hairs on your head are all
numbered. So don't be afraid; you are more valuable to him than a whole flock of sparrows."*

Because of our upbringing, circumstances or failures in life, many of us feel unwanted and worthless. Cutting remarks from others such as "You're useless!" ring in our ears. But God's Word shouts the opposite. You have value. You count! You are God's special creation, made in his image. And that is just the beginning of the story. God's Word is filled with covenant promises, redemption, grace, mercy, forgiveness, salvation, and guidance. All this is provided for you because God loves you and treasures you.

Regardless of painful circumstances or hateful words, know that you have value. Don't allow feelings of worthlessness to defeat you. Meditate on God's Word. Think about the fact that God created you with special care and loves you as his own. Let these truths sink into your soul, then bask in his love and live as his special child.

FOR FURTHER STUDY
• God has given you a position of great honor (Psalm 8:3-5).
  page 434

- You have been formed by God's loving hands (Isaiah 64:8). *page 576*
- God values all his creatures, especially people (Matthew 6:25-30). *page 734*
- You are of great value to God (Luke 12:4-12). *pages 796-797*
- God gave his Son for you (John 3:16). *page 814*
- Your relationship to Christ defines your self-worth (Romans 12:1-8). *page 875*
- Your self-worth is based on God's approval (2 Corinthians 10:12-18). *pages 898-899*

to overcome
SELFISH DESIRES

God's Word warns us not to be controlled by our selfish desires. Ephesians 4:21-24 tells us how:

> *Since you have heard all about him and have learned the truth that is in Jesus, throw off your old evil nature and your former way of life, which is rotten through and through, full of lust and deception. Instead, there must be a spiritual renewal of your thoughts and attitudes. You must display a new nature because you are a new person, created in God's likeness—righteous, holy, and true.*

When we surrender our hearts to God, God changes us from the inside out. Instead of seeking to satisfy our selfish desires, the Holy Spirit develops good desires and thoughts in us. First Peter 4:2 says:

And you won't spend the rest of your life chasing after evil desires, but you will be anxious to do the will of God.

Second Peter 1:4 outlines the necessity of God's power in our lives—we can only resist our selfish desires through his strength and power.

And by that same mighty power, he has given us all of his rich and wonderful promises. He has promised that you will escape the decadence all around you caused by evil desires and that you will share in his divine nature.

FOR FURTHER STUDY
- You should not desire something that belongs to someone else (Exodus 20:17). *page 63*
- Wicked people desire evil (Psalm 36:1-4). *page 448*
- God gives those who fellowship with him what they desire (Psalm 37:4). *page 449*
- Do not desire self-promotion (Psalm 119:36). *page 493*
- Money doesn't satisfy desires (Ecclesiastes 5:10). *page 528*
- Sinful desires should not have a home with God's children (1 Peter 1:14). *page 949*
- God's children desire to obey God (1 John 2:3-6). *page 956*

for SERENITY

Even in the necessary busyness of life, we can experience inner peace because we know we have been reconciled to God. Our right relationship with him gives us peace. Romans 5:1 reminds us of the true source of serenity.

Therefore, since we have been made right in God's sight by faith, we have peace with God because of what Jesus Christ our Lord has done for us.

Worrying about life's problems robs us of serenity. God wants us to pray about everything. He promises in Philippians 4:6-7 to give us peace and serenity if we trust him with thankful hearts.

Don't worry about anything; instead, pray about everything. Tell God what you need, and thank him for all he has done. If you do this, you will experience God's peace, which is far more wonderful than the human mind can understand. His peace will guard your hearts and minds as you live in Christ Jesus.

Serenity comes to those who are willing to slow down long enough to receive all God wants to give to them. The temple assistants who wrote Psalm 46:10 understood the secret to finding peace—be still in God's presence.

"Be silent, and know that I am God!"

Serenity is elusive in our fast-paced world. It's not easy to take the psalm writer's advice and "be silent." It's difficult to disengage, to slow down, and to listen to God. Thirsting for success and hungering for meaning, we push and strain and fill every waking moment with noisy activity. And we work hard to succeed in our own strength, in our own power, under our own control.

But this striving for success fills us with emptiness, not peace. Straining to achieve brings us disappointment, not serenity. True peace is found in the quiet moments we spend in God's presence.

God tells us to take a significant break from the frantic pace and hectic schedule, to move away from society's deafening cacophony, to stop talking and start listening to him. Then, and only then, will we be positioned to get to know him, our eternal, all-powerful, all-knowing, ever present God.

If you are searching for serenity, take the psalm writer's advice.

Be silent—listen to God's gentle whisper.
Be silent—know that he alone is your God.
Be silent—submit yourself to him.

FOR FURTHER STUDY
- Jesus is the Prince of Peace (Isaiah 9:6-7). *page 542*
- The peace Jesus offers is different than the world's peace (John 14:27). *page 828*
- Serenity is evidence of the Holy Spirit's work (Galatians 5:22). *page 906*

for SIMPLICITY

Jesus reveals the cost of discipleship in Luke 14:33. We must be willing to give up everything to follow God. The less we depend on worldly things, the more we can focus on spiritual things.

"No one can become my disciple without giving up everything for me."

Hebrews 13:5 warns us to be satisfied with what God gives us and to trust him to take care of our needs. Living simply demonstrates our dependence on God.

> *Stay away from the love of money; be satisfied with what you have. For God has said, "I will never fail you. I will never forsake you."*

FOR FURTHER STUDY

- A single focus on God is the path to peace (Isaiah 26:3). *page 551*
- Putting God's Kingdom first leads to simplicity (Matthew 6:31-34). *page 734*
- God calls to make his Kingdom our first concern (Luke 9:57-62). *page 793*
- Trusting God leads to simplicity (Philippians 4:11-13). *pages 914-915*
- Simplicity demands that you be content (1 Timothy 6:6-7). *page 927*

to resist SIN

David took a census of his army so that he could revel in the glory of his military strength. God used David's conscience to reveal his sin of pride and ambition. When we are sensitive to our consciences, we are better able to resist sin and repent of sin quickly. Second Samuel 24:10 says:

> *But after he had taken the census, David's conscience began to bother him. And he said to*

*the LORD, "I have sinned greatly and shouldn't
have taken the census. Please forgive me, LORD,
for doing this foolish thing."*

Sin begins in our minds. Jesus warned believers in
Matthew 5:27-28 that the first step in resisting sin
is to guard our thoughts.

*"You have heard that the law of Moses says, 'Do
not commit adultery.' But I say, anyone who even
looks at a woman with lust in his eye has already
committed adultery with her in his heart."*

We can receive great strength from Jesus Christ
to resist temptation. Though he never sinned,
Jesus faced trials and temptations. Hebrews 2:18
encourages us to turn to Jesus for help because
he understands our struggle against sin.

*Since he himself has gone through suffering and
temptation, he is able to help us when we are
being tempted.*

When Jesus became a living, breathing human
being, he became fully man with normal human
needs and desires. As a normal Jewish male, Jesus
experienced temptation. The Bible doesn't tell us
about his growing up years, but surely Jesus was
tempted to disobey Mary and Joseph, to assert
his independence, to lust, and to be filled with
pride. Later, after his public baptism by John the
Baptist, Jesus went into the wilderness where he
was tempted severely, alone, face-to-face with
Satan.

In all these temptations, Jesus struggled, he
suffered. Yet he did not give in to sin. He
remained pure.

What temptations entice you? The first-century
Jewish culture differs greatly from yours, but the

basic temptations are the same: lying, stealing, hatred, pride, self-indulgence, worshiping other gods, materialism, and many more.

Picture Jesus in your shoes, in your situation—how would he respond when offered the chance to cheat, to stretch the truth, to look at pornography? Ask him to help you resist sin. Then make the decision you think he would make.

FOR FURTHER STUDY
- Sin has consequences (Genesis 3:1-19). *pages 4-5*
- God must punish sin (Exodus 32:34). *page 74*
- You should humbly confess your sins to God (Ezra 9:5-15). *pages 389-390*
- You should ask God to forgive your sins (Psalm 51:1-10). *page 456*
- Stay away from people who lead you to sin (Proverbs 1:10-19). *page 507*
- All people have sinned (Romans 3:23). *page 867*
- Sin leads to eternal death (Romans 6:23). *page 870*
- Jesus takes the penalty of your sins on himself (Romans 8:1-2). *page 870*
- Sin begins with temptation (James 1:15). *page 945*
- You can sin by avoiding something that you should do (James 4:17). *page 947*
- God is willing to forgive your sins (1 John 1:8-9). *page 956*

for SPIRITUAL ARMOR

Evil is rampant in the world—we need more than our own strength to fight it. Ephesians 6:13-14 tells us that God gives us spiritual armor to help us resist temptation and live for him.

> *Use every piece of God's armor to resist the enemy in the time of evil, so that after the battle you will still be standing firm. Stand your ground, putting on the sturdy belt of truth and the body armor of God's righteousness.*

The spiritual armor God gives us *protects* us. Our salvation and faith can help us resist sin and remain strong in the Lord. First Thessalonians 5:8 admonishes believers to rely on their spiritual armor:

> *But let us who live in the light think clearly, protected by the body armor of faith and love, and wearing as our helmet the confidence of our salvation.*

FOR FURTHER STUDY

- You need to "put on" God's armor (Ephesians 6:11). *pages 910-911*
- God's armor helps you fight against evil (Ephesians 6:12). *page 911*
- God's peace is part of your spiritual armor (Ephesians 6:15). *page 911*

194

- Faith helps you resist Satan's attacks (Ephesians 6:16). *page 911*
- The Word of God serves as a spiritual sword (Ephesians 6:17). *page 911*

for SPIRITUAL GIFTS

Romans 12:6-8 outlines the kinds of spiritual gifts God gives to believers. This passage also emphasizes the importance of using our gifts to build up the body of Christ.

> *God has given each of us the ability to do certain things well. So if God has given you the ability to prophesy, speak out when you have faith that God is speaking through you. If your gift is that of serving others, serve them well. If you are a teacher, do a good job of teaching. If your gift is to encourage others, do it! If you have money, share it generously. If God has given you leadership ability, take the responsibility seriously. And if you have a gift for showing kindness to others, do it gladly.*

God is the source of all spiritual gifts. Ephesians 4:11-13 explains God's intentions in giving gifts— we are to use them in a way that helps others grow and mature in their faith. We should never use our gifts to draw attention to ourselves.

> *He is the one who gave these gifts to the church: the apostles, the prophets, the evangelists, and the*

*pastors and teachers. Their responsibility is to
equip God's people to do his work and build up the
church, the body of Christ, until we come to such
unity in our faith and knowledge of God's Son
that we will be mature and full grown in the Lord,
measuring up to the full stature of Christ.*

FOR FURTHER STUDY
- Spiritual gifts are given to build up the church (Romans
  12:3-5). *page 875*
- God gives spiritual gifts (1 Corinthians 12:4-11). *page 887*
- Spiritual gifts ought not be denied nor overemphasized
  (1 Thessalonians 5:19-22). *page 921*

for SPIRITUAL GROWTH

The community of believers, the church, is a good
place for believers to grow. As we serve faithfully
in the role God has given us in the church, he will
help us mature. Ephesians 4:16 describes how the
church should work:

*Under his direction, the whole body is fitted
together perfectly. As each part does its own
special work, it helps the other parts grow, so that
the whole body is healthy and growing and full of
love.*

Just as plants dig their roots deep into the soil for
nutrients, we should root ourselves in Jesus. We
draw strength and nourishment from him—Jesus

is the one who helps us grow strong and healthy. Colossians 2:7 gives us this picture:

> *Let your roots grow down into him and draw up nourishment from him, so you will grow in faith, strong and vigorous in the truth you were taught. Let your lives overflow with thanksgiving for all he has done.*

God knows better than anyone how we need to grow. Jeremiah 17:7-8 encourages us to trust God to put us in the best environment for us to mature.

> *"But blessed are those who trust in the LORD and have made the LORD their hope and confidence. They are like trees planted along a riverbank, with roots that reach deep into the water. Such trees are not bothered by the heat or worried by long months of drought. Their leaves stay green, and they go right on producing delicious fruit."*

A tree stands strong and green, bearing fruit year after year because a wise gardener planted it along a riverbank. Now its deep roots draw water from the life-giving stream that flows nearby.

In the same way, God knows what you need to nourish your soul—streams of living water—and he will plant you there if you let him. He will place you in the ideal environment for you to grow.

God's Word promises that those who put their hope in him will grow strong. Don't fear the heat or drought in your life; trust in the Lord. He will help you grow through the good and bad times.

FOR FURTHER STUDY
- God is the one who helps you grow (Colossians 2:19).
  page 917

for SPIRITUAL RENEWAL

Spiritual renewal comes from God alone—we must depend on him to change our hearts and lives. The psalmist's prayer in Psalm 51:10 is one we can bring before God with expectancy.

Create in me a clean heart, O God. Renew a right spirit within me.

Ephesians 4:22-24 emphasizes the necessity of spiritual renewal. We must be changed in our thoughts and attitudes to reflect God's likeness. God wants to make us holy for his glory.

Throw off your old evil nature and your former way of life, which is rotten through and through, full of lust and deception. Instead, there must be a spiritual renewal of your thoughts and attitudes. You must display a new nature because you are a new person, created in God's likeness—righteous, holy, and true.

FOR FURTHER STUDY
• Spiritual renewal begins with vision (Nehemiah 2:17-18).
  page 393
• Jesus set aside time for the spiritual renewal of his disciples (Mark 6:31). *page 766*

for STABILITY

God establishes his people, giving them deep
roots; he promises stability to the godly. Proverbs
12:3 says:

Wickedness never brings stability; only the godly
have deep roots.

Proverbs 28:2 assures us that if we seek God and
his wisdom, we will enjoy a level of stability that
this world can never provide.

When there is moral rot within a nation, its
government topples easily. But with wise and
knowledgeable leaders, there is stability.

FOR FURTHER STUDY
• Stability is found in God's unchangeable nature (Exodus
  3:13-15). *pages 47-48*
• Stability is found in moving with God (Numbers 10:21).
  page 119
• Friends come and go, but God remains forever (Job 12:4).
  page 417
• Your health may fail, but God remains your stability (Psalm
  73:26). *page 468*

- God is your stability, even in the face of temptation
  (1 Corinthians 10:13). *page 885*

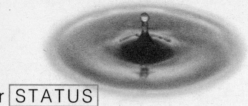

for STATUS

Galatians 2:6 teaches that God doesn't judge us according to our earthly status—our position and titles mean nothing to him. If God doesn't care about status, why should we?

And the leaders of the church who were there had nothing to add to what I was preaching. (By the way, their reputation as great leaders made no difference to me, for God has no favorites.)

James 2:2-4 warns against judging people because of their outward appearance. People's status and position should not impact our view of them or the way we treat them.

For instance, suppose someone comes into your meeting dressed in fancy clothes and expensive jewelry, and another comes in who is poor and dressed in shabby clothes. If you give special attention and a good seat to the rich person, but you say to the poor one, "You can stand over there, or else sit on the floor"—well, doesn't this discrimination show that you are guided by wrong motives?

FOR FURTHER STUDY
- Give up status to point others to Jesus (Matthew 3:15).
  page 731

to become good STEWARDS

Stewardship involves managing well the resources God gives us. Jesus, in Luke 16:10-12, assures us that if we use our money to honor God, he will honor us.

> *"Unless you are faithful in small matters, you won't be faithful in large ones. If you cheat even a little, you won't be honest with greater responsibilities. And if you are untrustworthy about worldly wealth, who will trust you with the true riches of heaven? And if you are not faithful with other people's money, why should you be trusted with money of your own?"*

First Timothy 6:17-18 warns of the dangers of becoming too dependent on our money. The best way to loosen money's grip is to give generously to God's work.

> *Tell those who are rich in this world not to be proud and not to trust in their money, which will soon be gone. But their trust should be in the living God, who richly gives us all we need for our enjoyment. Tell them to use their money to do good. They should be rich in good works and should give generously to those in need, always*

being ready to share with others whatever God has given them.

Wealth is a gift from God. Hebrews 13:16 encourages us to use our money to do good and help the needy. God is pleased with such self-sacrifice.

Don't forget to do good and to share what you have with those in need, for such sacrifices are very pleasing to God.

FOR FURTHER STUDY
- Generous giving honors God (Ezra 2:68-69). *page 383*
- Balance generosity and stewardship (Proverbs 6:1-5). *page 509*
- God blesses those who are responsible with their resources (Matthew 25:23). *page 754*
- God will reward you for giving to others (Mark 9:41). *page 770*
- Christians should support Christian workers (Acts 28:10). *page 863*
- Good stewardship honors God (1 John 3:17). *page 957*

for STRENGTH

In Psalm 23:3, David described God as a caring shepherd, one on whom he could depend for strength and guidance. In dark times, we should turn to God for strength.

He renews my strength. He guides me along right paths, bringing honor to his name.

Psalm 73:26 contrasts human weakness with God's strength. Our bodies are weak and *will* fail us, but God will *never* fail—he is our strength.

My health may fail, and my spirit may grow weak, but God remains the strength of my heart; he is mine forever.

FOR FURTHER STUDY

- God's strength has no limits (Numbers 11:23). *page 120*
- God does not want us to trust in our own strength (Judges 7:2). *page 204*
- Dealing with weaknesses enhances your strengths (Nehemiah 13:26). *page 404*
- God gives strength to his people (Psalm 18:32-34). *page 439*
- God is your source of strength (Isaiah 40:29-31). *page 562*
- Your perceived strengths can be your downfall (Obadiah 1:3). *page 700*
- Satan often attacks a person's strengths (Luke 4:3). *pages 784-785*

for help in dealing with STRESS

Paul endured intense stress and hardship on his missionary journeys. But he could see that through the stress and hardship, God was teaching him and his companions a valuable lesson: They were to rely on God and his power, not on themselves. Certainly, almighty God, "who can raise the dead," could be counted upon to rescue them from any "mortal danger." Second Corinthians 1:9-10 says:

> In fact, we expected to die. But as a result, we learned not to rely on ourselves, but on God who can raise the dead. And he did deliver us from mortal danger. And we are confident that he will continue to deliver us.

Paul faced many desperate situations. But whatever the situation, he could place his faith in God because he knew who God was and had seen God work before. Thus, he set his hope squarely on his awesome Lord and Savior. Second Corinthians 4:8-12 states:

> We are pressed on every side by troubles, but we are not crushed and broken. We are perplexed, but we don't give up and quit. We are hunted down, but God never abandons us. We get knocked down, but we get up again and keep going. Through suffering, these bodies of ours constantly share in the death of Jesus so that the life of Jesus may also be seen in our bodies. Yes, we live under constant danger of death because we serve Jesus, so that the life of Jesus will be obvious in our dying bodies. So we live in the face of death, but it has resulted in eternal life for you.

What stressful circumstances confront you today? Overwhelming responsibilities at work? Tension in your home? Lack of financial resources? Paul encourages you to learn what he had to learn the hard way—to rely on God.

Turn to your Father in heaven, even in your most desperate times. He "can raise the dead"; surely he can help you in your time of need.

Whenever you feel overwhelmed by the stress in

your life, give yourself a time out. Sit and think about those special times when God rescued you in the past, and believe that he will do it again. God "will continue to deliver" you. Turn to him—ask him to give you strength.

FOR FURTHER STUDY
- Delegating work can alleviate stress (Exodus 18:13-26). *page 61*
- God is a refuge in times of stress (Psalm 62:1-8). *page 461*
- Pray to God in times of stress (Psalm 69). *pages 464-465*
- Wait upon the Lord (Isaiah 40:30-31). *page 562*
- God is always with you (Romans 8:31-39). *pages 871-872*
- Don't let stress cause you to worry (Philippians 4:4-9). *page 914*

for SUCCESS

Uzziah was a successful king. God gave him success in war, in peace, and in all of his plans, but only as long as Uzziah relied on God for help. He experienced failure as soon as he took pride in his achievements, thinking he was the reason for his success. Second Chronicles 26:5 reveals:

> *Uzziah sought God during the days of Zechariah, who instructed him in the fear of God. And as long as the king sought the LORD, God gave him success.*

In contrast, Paul acknowledged God as the source of his success. In 2 Corinthians 3:5, he gave God credit for all of his achievements. Paul knew that he could do nothing of eternal value without the power of the Holy Spirit working through him.

> *It is not that we think we can do anything of lasting value by ourselves. Our only power and success come from God.*

Ecclesiastes 12:13-14 gives us an eternal perspective. In this summary to Solomon's chronicle of his search for meaning and purpose in life, he concludes that the secret of success is to "fear God and obey his commands."

> *Here is my final conclusion: Fear God and obey his commands, for this is the duty of every person. God will judge us for everything we do, including every secret thing, whether good or bad.*

From a human perspective, people should seek pleasure, wealthy, popularity, and power—these things bring success, according to the world. Solomon had achieved all of that and more; yet he summarized it all as meaningless, empty, vain. Solomon had learned that spending a lifetime pursuing worldly success just leads to moral and spiritual bankruptcy. It doesn't satisfy, and it fades as quickly as the morning dew.

But looking at life from beyond finite human experience, Solomon could see that, in reality, only God matters. So he implores us to "fear God and obey his commands."

No matter how you rate on the world's scale, focus on God and his standard. Success in his eyes is all that really matters.

FOR FURTHER STUDY
- God blesses those who seek to do right (Psalm 84:11).
  page 475

- Good advice helps to bring success (Proverbs 11:14). *page 512*
- Trusting everything to God leads to success (Proverbs 16:3). *page 515*
- Success in leadership is found through service (Matthew 20:26). *page 748*

for help in dealing with
SUFFERING

Christ's suffering enables him to help us in our times of suffering. Hebrews 2:17-18 reminds us that Jesus knows how we feel, he understands our pain, and he is *able* to help us.

> *Therefore, it was necessary for Jesus to be in every respect like us, his brothers and sisters, so that he could be our merciful and faithful High Priest before God. He then could offer a sacrifice that would take away the sins of the people. Since he himself has gone through suffering and temptation, he is able to help us when we are being tempted.*

When we follow Christ, we may suffer, just as Jesus did. First Peter 2:21 encourages us to follow Christ's example—he faced suffering with humility, patience, and quiet trust in God.

> *This suffering is all part of what God has called you to. Christ, who suffered for you, is your example. Follow in his steps.*

Revelation 21:4 offers great hope to those who are suffering. If we believe in the Lord Jesus, we will spend eternity in a place with no sorrow, tears, or pain. What a wonderful promise!

"He will remove all of their sorrows, and there will be no more death or sorrow or crying or pain. For the old world and its evils are gone forever."

FOR FURTHER STUDY
- Suffering is the result of sin (Genesis 3:1-19). *pages 4-5*
- God has compassion on his people when they suffer (Exodus 3:7). *page 47*
- Those who suffer need encouragement (Job 16:1-6). *page 419*
- Christ's followers will face suffering (Matthew 16:21-26). *page 745*
- Your suffering helps you comfort others in suffering (2 Corinthians 1:3-7). *page 893*
- Your suffering will end in glory (2 Corinthians 4:17-18). *page 895*
- Christ showed how to handle suffering (1 Peter 2:22-24). *page 950*

for SYMPATHY

Psalm 103:13 describes God as a gentle, merciful father who cares for the needs of his children. He is the ultimate source of comfort and sympathy.

The LORD is like a father to his children, tender and compassionate to those who fear him.

Hebrews 4:15 reveals that Jesus understands our pain because he experienced all of the trials and temptations that we will ever face. Go to the right source when you need sympathy.

> *This High Priest of ours understands our weaknesses, for he faced all of the same temptations we do, yet he did not sin.*

In Philippians 2:5-8, Paul reminds us that God is not aloof or removed from our struggles. He sympathizes with us in our difficulties. He loves us so much that he sent his own Son to take on human form to save us.

> *Your attitude should be the same that Christ Jesus had. Though he was God, he did not demand and cling to his rights as God. He made himself nothing; he took the humble position of a slave and appeared in human form. And in human form he obediently humbled himself even further by dying a criminal's death on a cross.*

It's easy to accuse God of not understanding our plight, especially when we hurt deeply and struggle for answers. God can seem so far away, so removed from the reality of our daily problems and questions. And during our pain we may question his love and justice.

But Scripture describes God as one who draws near to us and sympathizes with us. In fact, two thousand years ago, Jesus, the fully divine Son, humbled himself and became a man—a baby, totally dependent upon his parents for food and shelter—vulnerable, small, and weak. Like other children, the baby grew and matured to become a teenager and then an adult. Eventually, the Son's identification with us humans led to his suffering and death, for he was tormented, tortured, mocked, abandoned by his friends, and, finally, crucified. The least likely candidate, the innocent and pure Son of God, was executed as a notorious criminal.

Whatever your hurt, remember his. Not only does God understand, he sympathizes. He knows what you are going through—he lived it.

FOR FURTHER STUDY
- Jesus felt great sympathy for the needy (Matthew 9:36). *page 737*
- Jesus compassionately healed the sick (Matthew 14:14). *page 742*
- Jesus showed sympathy for the blind (Matthew 20:34). *page 748*
- Jesus truly sympathized with the family of Lazarus (John 11:35). *page 824*
- Believers should extend God's sympathy to others (1 Peter 3:8). *page 951*

to overcome TEMPTATION

In 1 Corinthians 10:13, God promises to show us a way to resist temptation. We should look for it!

> *But remember that the temptations that come into your life are no different from what others experience. And God is faithful. He will keep the temptation from becoming so strong that you can't stand up against it. When you are tempted, he*

will show you a way out so that you will not give in to it.

Wise people understand their weaknesses and do not underestimate the lure of sin. Paul encourages us in 2 Timothy 2:22 to run *away* from temptation *to* God.

> *Run from anything that stimulates youthful lust. Follow anything that makes you want to do right. Pursue faith and love and peace, and enjoy the companionship of those who call on the Lord with pure hearts.*

FOR FURTHER STUDY
- Temptation comes from Satan (Genesis 3:1-6). *page 4*
- Being careful to follow God's commands can help you avoid temptation (Proverbs 7:1-5). *page 510*
- Jesus was tempted but did not sin (Matthew 4:1-11). *page 731*
- Christ can help you, for he too has faced temptation (Hebrews 4:15-16). *page 936*
- God never tempts people to sin (James 1:13-15). *page 945*

for a THANKFUL HEART

Thankfulness should be a common thread woven through every aspect of our daily lives. Paul encourages us in Colossians 3:15-17 to pray and praise God with thankful hearts.

> *And always be thankful. Let the words of Christ, in all their richness, live in your hearts and make*

211

you wise. Use his words to teach and counsel each other. Sing psalms and hymns and spiritual songs to God with thankful hearts. And whatever you do or say, let it be as a representative of the Lord Jesus, all the while giving thanks through him to God the Father.

We can lose sight of God's goodness when we don't receive an answer to a long-standing prayer request. Thankfulness keeps us from forgetting about God's faithfulness while we are waiting for him to act on our behalf. Colossians 4:2 says:

Devote yourselves to prayer with an alert mind and a thankful heart.

Remember, thankfulness is a choice. If we choose to be thankful in all circumstances, God will give us peace. First Thessalonians 5:18 tells us it is God's will for us to be thankful.

No matter what happens, always be thankful, for this is God's will for you who belong to Christ Jesus.

FOR FURTHER STUDY
- Thank the Lord because he is good (Psalm 107:1-3). *page 487*
- Be thankful for God's unfailing love and faithfulness (Psalm 138:1-5). *page 501*
- Be thankful for salvation (Ephesians 2:4-10). *pages 907-908*
- Your prayers should include words of thankfulness (Philippians 4:6). *page 914*

for help in dealing with TRIALS

We are never alone when we face trials—Jesus promises his presence and strength. And we can claim God's peace, even in the face of overwhelming trials, because we know Jesus has won the victory over sin. His words in John 16:33 give us hope and courage:

"I have told you all this so that you may have peace in me. Here on earth you will have many trials and sorrows. But take heart, because I have overcome the world."

Everyone will experience trials—it's up to us whether we will learn from them or allow them to weaken our faith. James 1:2-4 challenges us to *welcome* trials because of the good they can do in our lives.

Dear brothers and sisters, whenever trouble comes your way, let it be an opportunity for joy. For when your faith is tested, your endurance has a chance to grow. So let it grow, for when your endurance is fully developed, you will be strong in character and ready for anything.

FOR FURTHER STUDY
- Christ promises rest from trials (Matthew 11:27-30). *page 739*
- Jesus understands your struggles (John 15:18). *page 828*
- Trials help to develop patience (Romans 5:1-5). *page 868*

213

- God knows what he is doing with your life (Romans 8:28). *page 871*
- Believers can expect to suffer for their faith (2 Corinthians 6:3-13). *page 896*
- Present trials fade in comparison to the joy of your relationship with Christ (Philippians 3:7-11). *page 914*

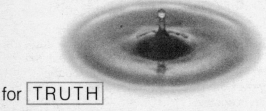

for TRUTH

Truth can seem elusive, but the Bible tells us in John 8:32 that Jesus holds the truth that sets people free.

> *"And you will know the truth, and the truth will set you free."*

While many people try to predict the future in an attempt to calm their fears, only one person holds the truth. Jesus assures us that the future of believers is secure. Take him at his word in John 14:1-4 and trust him with your future.

> *"Don't be troubled. You trust God, now trust in me. There are many rooms in my Father's home, and I am going to prepare a place for you. If this were not so, I would tell you plainly. When everything is ready, I will come and get you, so that you will always be with me where I am. And you know where I am going and how to get there."*

Jesus is God's truth, embodied in human form. John 14:6 acknowledges Jesus as the only path to the Father and to eternal life.

> Jesus told him, "I am the way, the truth, and the life. No one can come to the Father except through me."

Fear moistens our palms, buckles our knees, and chokes our breath. Debilitating fear makes cowards of even the strongest and most powerful warriors. Some try to fight their fears by ignoring them. Others mask their fears through anesthesia (alcohol and drugs) or false bravado (pretending that all is well). Some respond by rushing recklessly into danger. But the answer, the effective antidote to fear, comes from knowing the truth.

Jesus told his disciples that he was the Truth and that heaven awaited all who trusted in him. Thus they need not fear, regardless of their circumstances, pressures, and troubles. Certainly these young men didn't know the future, but they knew the One who did—and he promised them peace.

What fears steal your hope and keep you awake at night? Trust the Savior, and sleep like a baby.

FOR FURTHER STUDY
- Truth never changes (Proverbs 12:19). *page 513*
- God wants you to worship him in spirit and in truth (John 4:23-24). *page 815*
- God's Word is truth (John 17:17). *page 830*
- Be careful not to drift from the truth (Hebrews 2:1). *page 934*
- You must live out the truth (1 John 1:5-7). *page 956*
- Your actions demonstrate whether or not you are living in truth (1 John 3:19). *page 958*

for UNITY

Philippians 2:1-2 teaches that unity ought to be a distinctive mark among Christians.

Is there any encouragement from belonging to Christ? Any comfort from his love? Any fellowship together in the Spirit? Are your hearts tender and sympathetic? Then make me truly happy by agreeing wholeheartedly with each other, loving one another, and working together with one heart and purpose.

Jesus is the tie that binds! Racial, social, and financial distinctions are eliminated when people come to faith in Jesus Christ—he is the reason for our unity. Galatians 3:28-29 declares this truth:

There is no longer Jew or Gentile, slave or free, male or female. For you are all Christians—you are one in Christ Jesus. And now that you belong to Christ, you are the true children of Abraham. You are his heirs, and now all the promises God gave to him belong to you.

Differences divide families, neighborhoods, communities, and nations. Differences in race, nationality, culture, social status, language, and gender push people from each other. The news media continually report stories of civil unrest, hate crimes, bigotry, terrorism, and "ethnic cleansing." The more we become a global village, the more, it seems, we splinter and divide.

God's Word, however, describes a different situation. "In Christ Jesus" there is togetherness, oneness, unity. And instead of conflict, there is peace.

People of both sexes and all races, nations, and backgrounds are invited into God's blended family. Acceptance here is based only on Christ and what he has done. All who believe are welcome.

If you have ever felt the sting of prejudice and the loneliness of rejection, you know that this truth is good news! You are accepted and loved *now*, by God and your brothers and sisters, and you will live together in unity in heaven *then*.

FOR FURTHER STUDY
- Unity among believers pleases God (Psalm 133:1). *page 499*
- Christians are not supposed to live in isolation (John 17:11). *page 830*
- Unity includes bearing one another's joys and burdens (Romans 12:9-16). *page 875*
- Believers must seek unity in all essentials (1 Corinthians 1:10). *page 879*
- There can be great unity even in great diversity (Ephesians 4:3-13). *page 909*
- The love Christ commanded should create unity among believers (Philippians 1:3-11). *page 912*

to be USED BY GOD

First Corinthians 1:26-29 explains why God uses simple people to accomplish his work: so that he will receive all the glory he deserves. When we feel helpless and useless, we should offer ourselves to God, asking him to demonstrate his power through our weaknesses.

Remember, dear brothers and sisters, that few of you were wise in the world's eyes, or powerful, or wealthy when God called you. Instead, God deliberately chose things the world considers foolish in order to shame those who think they are wise. And he chose those who are powerless to shame those who are powerful. God chose things despised by the world, things counted as nothing at all, and used them to bring to nothing what the world considers important, so that no one can ever boast in the presence of God.

First Peter 5:5 teaches that God chooses to work through humble people. If you serve God with humility, he will use you to do great things for his Kingdom.

You younger men, accept the authority of the elders. And all of you, serve each other in humility, for "God sets himself against the proud, but he shows favor to the humble."

for WEALTH

Ecclesiastes 5:10 warns that craving wealth brings pain and anguish. The more we attain, the more we desire. We should avoid getting trapped in the vicious cycle of greed.

> *Those who love money will never have enough. How absurd to think that wealth brings true happiness!*

Thinking that wealth can make us happy is foolish. Only a right relationship with God brings fulfillment *and joy. Luke 12:21 says:*

> *[Jesus said] "Yes, a person is a fool to store up earthly wealth but not have a rich relationship with God."*

- Christians should not be lovers of money (1 Timothy 3:3). *page 925*
- Look to God for security, not wealth (1 Timothy 6:17-19). *page 927*
- Avoid the love of money (Hebrews 13:5). *page 943*

for WISDOM

Proverbs 1:7 reveals the first step in finding wisdom: fear of the Lord. He is the source of all wisdom.

> *Fear of the LORD is the beginning of knowledge. Only fools despise wisdom and discipline.*

God's wisdom is very different than the world's wisdom. First Corinthians 2:5-7 teaches that the "secret wisdom of God" is the message of salvation. We begin to receive God's wisdom when we accept Jesus Christ as our Savior.

> *I did this so that you might trust the power of God rather than human wisdom. Yet when I am among mature Christians, I do speak with words of wisdom, but not the kind of wisdom that belongs to this world, and not the kind that appeals to the rulers of this world, who are being brought to nothing. No, the wisdom we speak of is the secret wisdom of God, which was hidden in former times, though he made it for our benefit before the world began.*

James 1:5 offers hope to everyone thirsting for wisdom. James, under the inspiration of the Holy Spirit, promises us that God is eager to give us wisdom. The only thing we need to do is ask in faith.

> *If you need wisdom—if you want to know what God wants you to do—ask him, and he will gladly tell you. He will not resent your asking.*

Doubts assail like gale-force winds, tossing us this way and that. We wonder what to do, which way to turn, what direction to take. We may even question our faith, doubting God's goodness or even that he is there. Like night storms, difficult circumstances terrify us, confuse us, and fill us with anxiety. But God's truth cuts through the darkness like the powerful beam from a lighthouse, providing warning, direction, security, and hope.

We aren't abandoned to our doubts and uncertainties; God tells us to ask him for wisdom, and he will answer . . . "gladly."

Do you want to know what to do? Do you desire to follow God's way? Do you need his wisdom for the decisions you face?

Just ask in faith. He promises to give you his wisdom.

FOR FURTHER STUDY

- God's advice is always best (Psalm 73:24). *page 468*
- Wise people seek good advice (Proverbs 1:5). *page 507*
- To find wisdom, first find God (Proverbs 2:6-12). *pages 507-508*
- Wise people boast in knowing God (Jeremiah 9:23-24). *page 587*
- The wise follow God's guidance (Hosea 14:9). *page 690*
- The wise build their lives on God and his Word (Matthew 7:24-27). *pages 752-753*

to know how to WITNESS

Telling others about our new life in Christ is a privilege. In 2 Corinthians 5:18-19, Paul reminds us that we have a "wonderful message" to share. We should eagerly tell others!

All this newness of life is from God, who brought us back to himself through what Christ did. And God has given us the task of reconciling people to him. For God was in Christ, reconciling the world to himself, no longer counting people's sins against them. This is the wonderful message he has given us to tell others.

First Peter 3:15 encourages us to be ready to answer if someone asks us about our faith. We don't need to be an eloquent speaker to witness—just tell others what Christ has done for us!

Instead, you must worship Christ as Lord of your life. And if you are asked about your Christian hope, always be ready to explain it.

FOR FURTHER STUDY

- Sharing the Good News of Christ is beautiful (Isaiah 52:7). *page 570*
- God's message will accomplish what he desires wherever it is spoken (Isaiah 55:10-11). *page 571*
- Let your light shine (Matthew 5:14-16). *page 732*
- Jesus commanded all believers to witness (Matthew 28:16-20). *page 759*

- If you acknowledge your faith before people, God will acknowledge you (Luke 12:8-9). *page 797*
- Share the gospel with unbelievers (John 17:14-19). *page 830*
- Christians are called to spread the gospel across the world (Acts 1:8). *page 835*
- Believers plant or water the seed of faith, but only God makes it grow (1 Corinthians 3:5-9). *page 880*
- Unbelievers will not enter heaven (1 John 5:10-12). *pages 958-959*

for fulfilling WORK

Christians who work in the secular world may think that their work is not important. But 1 Corinthians 15:58 assures that our work can be used by God, if we do it enthusiastically for the Lord.

> *So, my dear brothers and sisters, be strong and steady, always enthusiastic about the Lord's work, for you know that nothing you do for the Lord is ever useless.*

Paul's instructions to slaves in Ephesians 6:5-7 encourage all believers to be responsible in their work. God is the one we should try to please; he is the one whom we are serving.

> *Slaves, obey your earthly masters with deep respect and fear. Serve them sincerely as you would serve Christ. Work hard, but not just to please your masters when they are watching. As slaves of*

Christ, do the will of God with all your heart.
Work with enthusiasm, as though you were work-
ing for the Lord rather than for people.

Paul admonished believers in Colossians 3:23-24
to do their work well, as an act of worship to the
Lord. We will find fulfillment in our work if we
remember that our ultimate boss is God.

Work hard and cheerfully at whatever you do, as
though you were working for the Lord rather than
for people. Remember that the Lord will give you
an inheritance as your reward, and the Master
you are serving is Christ.

Employers make mistakes. Bosses become bossy.
Supervisors reward incompetence. Teachers fail.
Mangers mismanage. That comes with living in a
sinful world with fallible, sinful human beings.

Regardless of the job or work situation,
however, God knows what's going on. He
perceives the attitude; he sees the work. He knows
whether someone is giving the best effort or just
getting by. Thus, God tells us we should work "for
the Lord rather than for people." Certainly this
would entail working hard, earning the wages,
and being honest.

Understanding whom we serve can also free us
from the trap of seeking earthly rewards and
acclaim. No amount of money can match God's
"inheritance," and no accolades can compare with
God's "Well done!" That awaits all who trust
Christ and serve him.

Regardless of the reactions of coworkers, class-
mates, and friends, focus on the Lord and work
for him. He will give you fulfillment and joy in
your work.

FOR FURTHER STUDY
• Work should not overrun your time with God (Exodus 16:23). *page 60*
• God gives you the ability to work (Exodus 35:30). *page 76*
• Christians should do their best at their job (Titus 2:9-10). *page 931*

to overcome WORRY

David's heart was heavy because a close friend had betrayed him. But instead of worrying, David released his fears and burdens to the Lord in prayer. In Psalm 55:22, he encourages us to do the same:

Give your burdens to the LORD, and he will take care of you. He will not permit the godly to slip and fall.

In Matthew 6:28-31, Jesus promises us that God will take care of our needs. We should trust him to keep his word. Trusting God includes not worrying.

"And why worry about your clothes? Look at the lilies and how they grow. They don't work or make their clothing, yet Solomon in all his glory was not dressed as beautifully as they are. And if God cares so wonderfully for flowers that are here today and gone tomorrow, won't he more surely care for you? You have so little faith! So don't

225

worry about having enough food or drink or clothing."

Food, drink, clothes—these comprise some of the basics of life. Why shouldn't we worry about them? No one wants to be hungry, thirsty, or unprotected.

The answer begins by understanding the difference between concern and worry. Concern means being aware of specific needs and then taking steps to meet those needs—concern leads to responsible action. It would be irresponsible and sinful, for example, for a father to be unconcerned about the basic needs of his family.

Worry, on the other hand, is extreme concern or an obsession with those needs. Filled with anxiety and fearing the worst, worriers nervously wonder about the future. They tend to spend more time filling their minds with ideas of the worst that could happen than working to make their dreams for the best that could happen come true.

The answer to the worry question is understanding that God is the ultimate source of everything good and that he loves us, knows our needs, and shares our concerns.

When tempted to worry about life's basic necessities, rely on this promise from Jesus: God will take care of you. As you live and work, trust him to meet your needs.

FOR FURTHER STUDY
- Worries fade away when we focus on God and his character (Psalm 37:7). *page 449*
- Worry weighs a person down (Proverbs 12:25). *page 513*
- Jesus says not to worry (Luke 12:22). *page 797*
- Don't worry about what you cannot control (Luke 12:26). *page 797*

- You don't need to worry, because God will meet all of your needs (Luke 12:29). *page 797*
- Don't worry about your place in life (1 Corinthians 7:21). *page 883*
- Pray instead of worry (Philippians 4:6). *page 914*
- Worry shows that you don't trust God (1 Peter 3:14). *page 951*

to WORSHIP GOD

God is present everywhere and always, so he can be worshiped at any time, in any place. The key is to worship him with sincerity and honesty. John 4:23-24 highlights the importance of genuine worship.

> *"But the time is coming and is already here when true worshipers will worship the Father in spirit and in truth. The Father is looking for anyone who will worship him that way. For God is Spirit, so those who worship him must worship in spirit and in truth."*

Worship draws our eyes off of ourselves, and focuses our hearts on God. He alone is holy and awesome—he deserves our praise and worship. Hebrews 12:28 reveals that our worship pleases God.

> *Since we are receiving a kingdom that cannot be destroyed, let us be thankful and please God by worshiping him with holy fear and awe.*

FOR FURTHER STUDY
- Worship is an encounter with the living and holy God (Exodus 3:1-6). *page 47*
- Worship is reserved for God alone (Exodus 34:14). *page 75*
- In worship, believers ascribe to the Lord the glory due him (Psalm 29:1-2). *page 444*
- Music is useful to focus worshipers' attention on God (Psalm 81:1-2). *page 473*
- Make music for God's glory (Colossians 3:16). *page 918*
- You can worship because of Christ's sacrifice on your behalf (Hebrews 10:1-10). *page 940*
- When you draw near to God in worship, he draws near to you (James 4:8). *page 947*